MW01126051

# Born
## to
# Flirt

*Helen Parui*

# BORN to FLIRT

⋙ A MEMOIR ⋘

# HELEN PARIS

SHADOWRIDGE PRESS

BORN TO FLIRT
First published March 2017
by Shadowridge Press

Copyright © 2017 by Helen Paris
All rights reserved.

Book layout and design by Robert Barr

ISBN: 978-1-946808-07-3

shadowridgepress.com

# Born to Flirt

# PROLOGUE

This story is about a large family, its successes and its tragedies. It starts in the mid1920s during the Flapper fun times beginning with my grandmother who was a smart, hard-working woman with only one child. She, as did her forerunners and descendants, turned out to be "Born to Flirt" with the world around them.

# But First …

## A Brief Word from My Guardian Angel …

Just when I thought things had evened out for you—you've gotten rid of a few bad habits and negative relationships—here comes this thing about ancestors. I tell you, being your Guardian Angel is no small job. But don't panic, I'll help.

To make it a little easier, you will be glad to know that they all made it. None of them were consistently bad enough to go to the other place. So, that gets you off to a good start.

A small problem, but still a problem; very few of them stayed married to the same person for any length of time. It's hard to track folks like that down. Then, too, since you didn't know your father and didn't want to stir up your mother by asking too many questions, his family sort of stayed in the lost and found column. Remember your mother calling them "Shanty Irish"? That really bothered you. Funny, it wouldn't bother you at all now. There's something to be said for getting old, I guess.

You do remember hearing about Leta, don't you? She was your father's sister and, when you did something really bad, you were supposed to be just like her. Poor Leta!

The ones you did know were pretty interesting folks. You didn't know your great grandparents, but they had to have been wonderful people. Remember Great Aunt Kit talking about them?

Aunt Kit, Uncle Frank, Uncle Ned and Gramma were brothers and sisters. They all loved each other dearly, they really cared. So, that's where all of this family love came from, I suppose. Their parents were named Searl but their mother's maiden name was DeLacey. You always loved that name. Perhaps you'll write a novel some day with characters named Hallie and Paris DeLacey. Think about it.

As you know, most of your folks came from France (those that weren't Shanty Irish). I suppose they started with your great, great grandparents because they settled in Ohio around Cleveland, Toledo and Ravenna. They stayed there, too, until your Gramma moved to Atlanta.

She was one cute lady, smart, good looking, feisty, and so full of energy that she could direct most any way she pleased—very independent, but caring. She ended up looking after everyone. You all had your turn living with her for a while during your growing up years. You called it your finishing school.

She married your mother's father, Howard Smith. He was a nice enough, very successful man but apparently not what Gramma wanted because she divorced him before your mother was fully grown and married Doc Smellie, who had six children. She was a daring lady who followed her heart and it worked!

Your Great Aunt Kit, Gramma's sister, was a "sport." She didn't marry until she was fifty. However, she married well. Even though love came late to Aunt Kit, she was happy.

Remember when you were fourteen and went to live with Gramma and Doc? Well, Aunt Kit lived there also. And even though she was old, she was fun. You both liked the same movies and ice cream, played rummy and solitaire together. The most exercise she got was from pushing those cards around. But she lived to be ninety-seven years old. If she hadn't broken her hip, I guess she would still be living, such a good-humored lady.

There are plenty of relationships for you to write about but you couldn't call them ancestors yet. Actually you have as many ancestors as anyone else, the difference being your folks didn't keep track of them. Now, the thing for you to do is to keep on writing about every relative that you know so that our children and their children's children have the line that will have some ancestors, us.

# PART
# ONE

*1917-1967*

CHAPTER
# ONE

## Hallie and the Early Years

"Extra! Extra! Prominent woman chiropractor critically injured by hit and run driver!"

Newsboys hawked their papers loud and clear on street corners throughout Atlanta on September 12, 1924, a day that would not soon be forgotten by the family of that hit-and-run victim, Dr. Helen Searl Smith Smellie. Hallie (as she was always known to friends and family) suffered injuries that were serious and permanent. She lost one eye and had internal injuries plus a broken hip and other broken bones. For several days, she was not even expected to live.

By today's standards, Hallie was born liberated. Besides being petite and beautiful, there was never a question as to her independence as a person. She was a DeLacey through and through. DeLacey, her mother's maiden name, was of French origin even though her father was English. Her brothers, Ned, the oldest, and Frank, the youngest, and her sister Catherine (known variously as Kit, Kate, and Katie) were all bright, good, upstanding children, but Hallie was the leader from the beginning. She was strong, she was smart, and she could always find the answers. They learned early on to depend on her. She loved it and so did they. She was the original free spirit, not afraid of new experiences and not especially interested in other people's opinions of her. She became a school teacher at nineteen and sometime later a dance instructor.

In 1873 Hallie fell in love with Howard Smith, a handsome young man with a promising future in the business world. They had one daughter, Margaret, a beloved child who sometimes got in their way. They gave her every advantage, in the way of private schools and the like, and they really loved her in their busy way. Howard was always a bit vague and Hallie so very positive. Hallie and Howard's marriage, though not perfect, was never violent. It simply fell apart when Margaret became an adult and was married.

The rumor has it that Hallie met and fell madly in love with Alexander Baxter Smellie while still married to Howard. He was a fast moving, handsome, most persuasive man with six precocious children. That did not deter Hallie, who took them all in stride, divorced Howard, and married her darling "Sandy." What a romance that was! It lasted until the death of Sandy forty years later.

They first met at the Battle Creek Chiropractic School, drawn to each other because they were both very clever, beautiful people. Hallie became one of the first female chiropractors in Atlanta—possibly the very first—and definitely made the most of her practice.

Sandy's children from his first marriage were an outgoing bunch. They loved Hallie and played by the rules of the house but they had a separate little clique going together. Baxter, the eldest, died, which left beautiful Marda as their second mother. She certainly filled the void left by her mother in the best possible way. Winston (Win) and Ronald (Ron) were close in age, only two years apart and so inseparable that they were always known as Win-and-Ron rather than by their individual names. Tamara (Tommie) was next, a good looking and friendly tomboy. Finally there was the baby, Elizabeth (Betty), so feminine and lovely and a bit spoiled by all.

Hallie's own daughter Margaret, who was a determined, headstrong, Garbo look-alike, met and fell in love with Donald Oldham at an early age. She was married at eighteen and had her first child, a boy named Howard Donald, one year later. And so her busy—and, as far as love went, tragic—adult life began. Her parents felt, and probably for good reason, that she had not married wisely. They were not fond of Donald Oldham but as usual accepted any and every thing that Margaret did with a fair amount of grace, hoping that this time they were wrong. Not so. Donald's large family was working class Irish, not especially aggressive. He had several brothers, as well as a sister named Leta whom Margaret did not like one little bit.

All of this occurred during World War I. Donald was too young to be called up when America entered the war, and apparently either poor health or being the father of several children kept him from being called up at all. He and Margaret had their second child, Helen, in 1917 and three years later along came number three, a beautiful baby boy with red curly hair. He was a darling but for some reason was not named for several years, being known only as Angel. Actually, the marriage had started falling apart before Angel's birth. So perhaps that was the reason for the delay.

Donald's health deteriorated suddenly and in a way that no one understood, least of all Margaret. He became disoriented and unpredictable, often violent toward Margaret. They lived in Toledo, Ohio, while Hallie, who had just married Sandy, moved to Atlanta. So there was Margaret alone, with three small children, no money, and frightened out of her mind by her husband. After struggling, trying desperately to find an answer for several months, she left Donald in the middle of the night while he slept. Helen and Sandy had sent her money, enough to get to Atlanta by train.

Helen and Sandy were doing quite well. They lived in a big, comfortable house with plenty of room for their large family of four teenagers. (Marda had moved to Chicago, since she was older, and had met and fallen in love with a fine man named Harry Cain, who was studying to be a chiropractor and seemed to have a good future. It turned out to be true because later they married and had a happy life.)

Even though Hallie and Sandy welcomed Margaret and her brood, their coming did stretch the bedroom space and the budget. The four children, Win and Ron, Tommie and Betty, were kind to Margaret and her children but it was different for them to have to consider younger children who loved to snoop into their dresser drawers and their closets. Tempers flew on occasion.

Margaret soon found employment as a telephone operator with Southern Bell, then later with a downtown grocery store named Kemper's. She loved her work. She was a telephone operator—took grocery orders, I believe, and put them on a pulley of some sort to send them on their way to be delivered.

They were a sophisticated family. They worked hard and played hard—golf, tennis, swimming, all of the competitive sports. They all loved to dance. As they grew older, since all four of them were near the same age, they had mutual friends and a good time was had by all.

Hallie never tried to take their mother's place in their hearts but was always there, the strength of the family, and everyone sensed it. She was a beautiful, independent, busy person, always learning and never too busy to teach, but she ruled her family in her quiet, determined way. Her children did not ever think of disobeying— except for Margaret.

# CHAPTER
# TWO

## To Courtland Street

She laid the baby wrapped in blankets down into the snow so that she could lock the door securely behind us. She actually locked that part of her life out forever, as well as locking it out of mine and my two brothers. My mother was running away from my father in the middle of the night as he slept.

The very first house in my young memory belonged to my beloved Gramma in Atlanta, Georgia, and was a pretty white one on a corner lot with a lovely soft green lawn. It was late winter or early spring when we left Toledo, Ohio for Atlanta, so the unexpected green grass and blooming flowers impressed me.

My grandmother and step-grandfather made room for us, even though they had four teenagers of their own. My grandmother had fallen in love with this beautiful family of six children and their most handsome, personable father. It was a marriage of true love "until we both shall die."

I was not quite four, so I don't remember every detail. It just felt happy there. We slept upstairs and I'm sure the teenage boys and girls (there were two of each) had to double up to fit us in but, since this was a happy home with great discipline, we all felt wanted.

It seems that I am not remembering the actual building so much as the atmosphere. This house was made up of love and order. I felt safe. And, as you will see, that feeling was part of me for as long as Gramma lived.

I remember the living room as being big and airy, most pleasant. Each night we all had dinner together, everyone had their own napkin rings. And when we finished eating, we folded our cloth napkins and put them back into the rings for the next meal. Everyone knew their own ring.

Before dinner sometimes, I'm sure not every night, my tall, handsome, smiling and probably young step-grandfather would call my brother, Billy, and me (we were almost four and six) to fold a few old newspapers. And out we would go to the neighbors to sell them. That was so much fun because the neighbors had been alerted and had their pennies ready. And so, we earned our dinner.

We called my step-grandfather "Doctor," as did all of the family except his children. He and my grandmother were chiropractors and had been for years, having met, as I said, while in school in Battle Creek, Michigan. Hallie, my grandmother, was a very cultured, brilliant person so I think Doctor had to have been a love for this beautiful, vibrant woman to take him breakfast in bed every morning. His favorite food was a fried banana, and I remember trotting up the stairs behind Gramma with that delicious tray—I always got a taste. We could have all had fried bananas, I suppose, but that was something special for Doctor.

Billy and I were probably pretty good kids, but we found out that the chest in the upstairs hall was the hiding place for Win and Ron's gum and candy. So, of course, we got into the good stuff. That's the only time I remember the boys fussing at us. They were called "the boys" and Tommie and Betty were called "the girls."

Those few months were probably melded deep into my mind and soul as being what a loving, stable home should be like because very soon things would change and I would have another house to remember.

This house was different. Even though I was still just a little girl not yet five, I remember the location, the structure, the neighborhood and even a few people associated with this ugly house on Courtland Street. The particulars of this move were never explained to me, so I was a pretty bewildered child. It seemed to me that out of the clear air along came this strange man whom we were supposed to call "Daddy".

We moved out of my grandmother's lovely home into a duplex. We had one side and the other was a photographer's studio belonging to the strange man my mother had married. The duplex was located near the corner of Courtland and Ellis Street. That section wasn't as bad then as it became later but it was not good. The house was run down and we had a minimum of furniture, just beds and absolute necessities.

I can see all of this in my mind's eye. It was built close to the street with broken brick side walls. As you stepped up about six rickety steps to the front porch, you entered a long hall partitioned off by a curtain about midway down. My brother and I slept in back of that curtain on some kind of a cot. The front room on one side was on the left, and back of that, shotgun style, was a bedroom, then a bath of sorts and straight back was a kitchen of which I have no memory. The studio side of the house was always smelling of the chemicals used in the dark room. On its side of the porch was a big shadowbox window showcasing my stepfather's pictures, which were mostly of the Ku Klux Klan. I later learned that he was one of the Klan's official photographers. That might not have been so bad for a studio, but for a home?

We had some interesting neighbors—I just wasn't old enough to appreciate what it all meant. Next door was a large, two-story house with a big front porch filled with rockers and swings, that I thought was so pretty. Early in the evening all of these pretty ladies would come out to sit and rock, or so I thought. They loved me and would invite me over. They would talk to me and just treat me special, so I enjoyed myself. I later found out that they were ladies of the evening.

Even though I did not like this particular house, some good things did happen from time to time. My grandmother did not desert us. Since my mother worked—she was a telephone operator—

Gramma would find time to come by in the morning and bathe and feed us. And to talk and play with us. I remember she told me to always scrub the spot in back of my shoulder blade. Of course, I couldn't reach it. Why do I remember that?

Another nice thing about living in this house was that the Marist School was located one street over and every Sunday morning they had band practice. We could hear them loud and clear and would march and dance all morning. I also remember how much fun it was to read the Sunday funnies.

To add a little mystery to this house, in the back of us—our back yards joined—lived a delightful lady artist. I thought at the time she was old, but she probably wasn't. Her name was Mrs. Drew and she was quite well known in Atlanta. Like my stepfather, she too had her studio in her house, so maybe that neighborhood was Artists Row at that time. Besides oil painting, she sculpted and at one point she insisted on sculpting Billy in the nude in her garden. He kicked and screamed all the way, but it got done. Mrs. Drew was so nice and sincere, and she really liked children. I wish I had kept in touch with her in later years when I could have, but I suppose I forgot about her for a while. Only years later when I read in the magazine section of the Sunday paper that she had been murdered by her yard man did I remember all of this. She was a real dear. Even though she didn't sculpt me in her garden, she did let me wash her dishes each Saturday morning. She would tie me up in a huge apron, stand me up on a box by her sink and let me go at it. She didn't care how many dishes I washed or how I did it, she just let me have fun. I would eat Vanilla Wafers, the ones she got out for me, and then she would give me the whole box. I'm going to look into her murder. She was so well known, I'm sure someone remembers, Celestine Sibley maybe.

I was very mixed up about that strange man who became my stepfather. I didn't like him and I don't believe he liked me or my brothers. I suppose my life was a little spooky for a small girl. The strange man had an Overland touring car that had cloth and celluloid curtains that snapped or pulled down in some way. I remember one time going out to Stone Mountain. It was dark. When we got there, the Ku Klux Klan was doing whatever they did—burning crosses and ranting and the like—and, since our stepfather was the official photographer of the Klan, we got a real close-up view of all of the happenings. My brother and I were scared to death. We hid down on the floor of the car, hoping we would get out alive.

Then there was the Jelly Coal Man. He would come by in a horse and wagon singing his wares. And the Ice Man too, who also had a wagon, a horse drawn one, I believe. Anyway, he had great big tongs that he carried the ice into the house with. You could order ten or twenty pounds, whatever you wanted, and he would chip it off expertly. While he was doing all of this, we would get little chips of ice to eat. Some of the big kids would climb into the wagon and get big chunks. And there was the organ grinder man who had a crank organ and a monkey to collect pennies. We nearly died of excitement when he came. The monkey was so cute, dressed up, always wore a little hat. I only remember these people when we were in the Courtland Street house.

Between our house and the "ladies" house my brother and I had a little cardboard store that we had put together out of boxes. We were experts at making mud pies and would leave them out to dry. Well, one night the police were chasing a drunk and, would you believe, the drunk ended up in our little store trying to sell mud pies to the cops.

Across the street and up an alley was the black community where one of the people who kept us while our mother was working lived. I suppose she got tired of our food because one day she took us to her house and we sat down to the best food I have ever had. That was my introduction to Soul Food.

We only lived on Courtland for about one year but we had lots of experiences. I couldn't have been more than five, but before we moved I went to some kind of school. Billy was two years older, so he was in real school. We walked and had to go by a bottling plant, Nu-Grape, I believe. There was so much talk about prohibition that we didn't understand. But this one thing we did know; whatever it was, it was evil. So, when we passed by the bottling plant and heard the machines rattling the bottles, we really moved. We must have been live-wires with big imaginations.

One night my mother and a friend took me to see Peter Pan at the Loew's Grand. Since we were close, we walked. On the way home my mother suddenly picked me up and ran all the way home. Shortly after that Gramma put us, my brother and me, in a private boarding school. I don't remember how long we lived there or the name of the lady who ran it. I just know it was one Easter and my birthday because we had an Easter breakfast. It wasn't so bad but we were bewildered. Back then folks didn't tell kids a whole lot. But I later figured things out. My mother had run that night because a man was following us, and that man was my father, hence the reason for hiding us.

The reason I don't mention my baby brother Angel very often is because I'm not sure he was with us all the time. I wonder if my grandmother had him. I'm sure he wasn't in the boarding school. I remember taking him to the corner store when he was just starting to walk. The clerk or owner thought he was cute and gave him an apple, but did not give me one. So I took one. What shame I was made to feel by that man. I hid it under my arm, or so I thought. How could a little girl hide an apple under her arm? I guess my crime made an impression on  me because I've thought about it often, and I will say I've never stolen another apple.

I guess you can tell I remember very little about the boards and walls of this house. My mother was there, but I don't remember much about her, just a few incidents. We sound like pretty independent kids, don't we? Funny how it all turned out okay.

While we're still on Courtland Street, I will tell you about an incident that has stayed in my mind as though it happened last night. The only part that is not clear is his face. One night as I was taking a bath in walked in the man that my mother had married, along with another man.  They were talking and laughing, really not paying too much attention to me. The man just wanted to go to the bathroom. He looked at me and hesitated. I'm sure he felt strange doing this thing with a little girl in the bath tub. As he hesitated, my stepfather said, "Don't mind her, it doesn't matter." So, the man proceeded, quite an education for me.

My stepfather was divorced from his first wife and had three children, older than we were. I later got to know the two boys (the girl died during childbirth) but can only really remember the young-est. His name was Jack, and he was cute as could be but a devil towards us. I remember when he came to visit his father, he would pick on us good.

# CHAPTER
# THREE

## LIVING IN POVERTY

Shortly after my mother married the photographer, our family moved to Melbourne, Florida.

They were both young and had high hopes, I suppose, of building a life together down there, but it seemed that we became poor the moment we stepped off the Dixie Flyer in Melbourne, leaving behind in Atlanta my beloved grandmother and all of her stability. (A few years later, when the depression really hit, it seemed to make no difference to our family; we were already poor as could be). I was about six years old when we arrived and that was my first taste of unhappiness. My mother had had her good job with Kemper's Grocery Store in Atlanta, but there was no job in Melbourne and before long there were three more children to care for.

Until I was fourteen we lived in poverty. Looking back, I suppose it was harder on the adults than on the children. Our grandmother sent us money for food most every week. And when she didn't, she got a telegram collect asking for it. For the first three years she sent boxes of clothes and toys and beautiful books for Christmas.

We had a good school in Melbourne, the only drawback being

that we had to buy our own books. I believe they were furnished in the lower grades. Later on when my younger brother and sister got in school, breakfast and lunch were also furnished for the first few grades. That was a good program—at least part of the family got fed. However, they were self- conscious about it because you had to be poor enough, and everyone knew it. My little brother, John Jr., seemed to mind it the most. I'm sure we ate the kind of food that made or kept us pretty healthy. We had grits and rice—made by a Yankee mother from Ohio who put diluted canned milk and sugar in them—and pork and beans. Different years brought some different foods. My stepfather became a big-time fisherman, not to make money at it, but he was the big sport and belonged all of the civic clubs. Anyway, we had fish. I remember sometimes we simply did not have anything to eat before we went to bed. So, since he fished at night, they would wake us up late at night, knowing we were hungry. Sometimes they were out of kerosene to cook inside, so they would build a wood fire in the yard.

My mother must have let it be known through the Welfare Committee in Melbourne that possibly some of her children might be up for adoption, mainly the three oldest. A couple who lived nearer into town in a nice white house very near the grammar school offered to adopt my brother Bill, the oldest. It was discussed in our family—I don't remember my stepfather being included in these talks, just my mother and we children—but it did not go through; either the couple backed out or my mother did.

Now I realize that she was in a very bad situation. She had to be madly in love with my stepfather to put up with all of the things she did. I know she realized that we, the three oldest, were not his and that was the problem; we were simply in the way. And yet, no doubt, she loved us in her way. During her angriest moments we were threatened with being sent to an orphanage. We never really believed it, so it didn't bother us too much. But she had to think, "What have I done? My marriage is being ruined because of too many children." She had six in all, three of us she brought into her marriage, no doubt thinking it would work. We knew nothing about it until she told us to call him "Daddy." Oh, Lord, have pity on us, the three little babies. We were so small and innocent. Angel (Hal) was a baby about eighteen months and Bill and I had to be around four and five. What a shock that had to be for us. From the very beginning we were ignored by him and we understood, as only small children can, that our job was to stay out of the way and please him.

My mother had to trust him completely to go to Melbourne and to start what she thought was the perfect life. Little did she know it just meant three more children, a number of miscarriages and poverty for years to come. I suppose we were so confused and resentful thinking, "There is something better out there," that we did not stop to realize how hard it was for our mother. Even though she yelled and hit much of the time, she still seemed to keep a sense of humor just enough to pull us out of the deep.

All we kids managed to grow up one way or another, and not one of us could deny her strength or bravery. Needless to say, it was a tough way to become an adult, but when we did we were all able to laugh and joke through our tears.

We all made mistakes, some had harder lives than others but all of us were strong. We were successful in many ways. We had good marriages – two of my brothers had to keep trying but won out in the end—and raised fine beautiful families. I had better modify that a bit. Brother Bill messed up at first; he never kept up with his first wife and two children, which wasn't good. Brother John didn't have children and married his wife twice but ended up happy. She died a contented woman, I believe.

Franklin Delano Roosevelt defeated Herbert Hoover when the country was really wobbling. FDR was the people's idol. He gave us hope, inspired folks to work at anything. He founded the CCC, Civilian Conservation Corps, that gave jobs to many men. They built national parks, mountain resorts, many roads. Welfare was started to help feed and clothe many. Soup kitchens sprung up. We didn't have any of these in Melbourne but we heard about them, and I suppose young men from Melbourne benefited from all of this.

Except for not having a good living we got along all right. But I know of other families that fared much better, perhaps because they worked together, which my mother and her husband did not.

We were what is now called a dysfunctional family.

As I got older I made friends with some girls that came from very well-to-do families. Everyone in Melbourne was not poor by any means. Lots of times I was invited to eat a meal with their families. Come to think of it, we were probably the poorest people around. But there were many more in even worse shape in the cities and out on the farms. I understand that the average farmer only netted $172.00 per year.

But even so children were safe to be out and about as they pleased. I guess the most crimes were committed by children. It was just accepted that we all stole oranges off of trees in yards. It made folks kind of mad but that was not a sin, it was a sport.

Polio was the dreaded disease back then. It crippled President Roosevelt as a young man. Many children died or were crippled. Antibiotics had not been discovered. We had no refrigeration as we know it now, just ice boxes, had an ice truck come door to door as we moved about. We very seldom had electricity. The Rural Electric Administration was a great help to the farmers. The WPA, Work Progress Administration, gave work to many. I was a little young to be aware of all that went on. But Roosevelt started the communication between government and people by having what were called "Fireside Chats." He encouraged everyone to do the best they could. He had the most charisma of any President we have ever had in my mind.

The Depression brought about different types of music, some silly, some happy, like when Roosevelt got the economy moving a bit, "Happy Days Are Here Again." Everyone sang that song.

Some folks had automobiles, but many did not. Our across the road neighbor had a truck with cork tires. They wore out but never were flat. We got a lot of exercise; we walked everywhere we went.

Movies were silent, black and white, had musicians playing down front in a pit. When Tom Mix was on, they played horse music, when it was a love scene, they played love music, and so on. It cost a nickel to go to the picture show in Melbourne, so we didn't go often. You could walk down the street on a Friday or Wednesday night and know what time it was because Amos and Andy or Kate Smith came wafting out of service stations or homes with radios.

Life was not all bad, especially if you were young and knew that that was not all there was. We had churches that had a few activities, not many, but some. They got up Thanksgiving baskets and left them on your doorstep, so as not to embarrass you.

We had a good school spirit, great football team and basketball team, and a really quite good band. I loved to be walking home after school later when everything was quiet and hear the school band practicing or the football team practicing, I loved the sounds.

⁂

The part of Melbourne that our family lived in was made up of tall pine trees, palmettos everywhere, blazing sun, snakes, a few skunks, sandspurs, poison oak and deep rutted, back woods, sandy roads. If you were fortunate enough to have a car, heaven help you if you got out of those ruts and got stuck in the sand. The only way to get out was to put a flat board under your back wheels, unless you were smart enough to just let a little air out of the back tires.

It seemed to me that we were always walking. Our stepfather had a broken down, one-seated car that no one but him rode in. He had such an undeserved ego. He was a member of all of the civic clubs in this little town, Rotary, Anglers, Chamber of Commerce, etc. He had a cot in his studio and that's where he slept. Never did I see his clothes in our house. However, he was around enough to keep those babies coming.

All of this ugliness was transformed when the sun went down. Everything was dark except Florida's beautiful sky. It seemed to me that the moon was always full, the Milky Way and the stars so near. I could actually read by the light of the moon from my bedroom window.

The runny-nosed, sore-infected, fighting, crying, dirty children turned into peaceful sleeping angels. I always had two or three of them sleeping with me and they were sweet children, never mind that before morning I would be soaking wet thanks to one or all of them.

On the rare occasions when my stepfather was home he would turn on his radio late at night. I don't remember much about that radio, it could be that he brought it back and forth from his studio.

Anyway, no one could touch it. I do remember the music and, since my bedroom was an open area at the top of the stairs, I could hear it like it was in my room. What else would a ten or eleven-year-old girl do but dance? The floors creaked and my stepfather yelled. So, I would stop for a while and then start back. I loved to dance in the moonlight.

This particular house was badly infected with bed bugs and roaches. I don't know what attracted them because there was nothing to eat but us—we ate all of the crumbs. The way we slowed the bed bugs down was to take the bed springs and mattresses outdoors, torch the springs with burning paper and pick them out of the mattresses with needles and pins. We didn't relish that job.

We moved a lot. Sometimes when we were about to be evicted we moved at night. Our mother was an enterprising woman.

Our neighbors in this particular neighborhood were all very good people. The Van Lenghams had nine children, so we never ran out of someone to play with. Their parents were old and stooped— or maybe they weren't so old and we just thought they were. They had children from thirty to six years old. Ann was the baby, Martha was my friend, Hank and Eddie were my brother's friends. Ben was perhaps eighteen and he got mixed up with a grown man who drove a big black car. Sometimes they would let us ride in it. I was too young to know what was going on, but I do remember my mother making little remarks, so I knew something was not right. Old Man Van Lengham, as we called him, had a bakery in his back yard. The wonderful, delicious smells that came out of that house were something. I remember they had a manual machine that wrapped loaves of bread and, since all of the kids worked in the bakery, sometimes they would let me go in and watch Martha wrap bread. I believe he was a talented baker because he had a pretty good business until he developed tuberculosis. That was bad because he was forced to give up his business. However, they turned it into a laundry and again had a decent living.

I loved it when every now and then they would ask me to eat. What an experience! They had a pretty nice house, electricity, a wall clock and a long dining room table with benches on each side. Lots of good food, meat, potatoes, the best hash browns in the world. Sometimes I would spend the night with Martha. Each child had a curtained off space just large enough for a bed, but that space was theirs. They had a big chamber pot in the hall for everyone to use. Each child took turns emptying it the next day.

These nights were fun. We would play jackstones until bedtime or jump board, pretty dangerous because I was so small and Martha larger. Each of us would get on one end of a long limber board supported in the middle by a large rock and take turns jumping, send the other high off the board. The trick was in landing back on the board. We got pretty good. The best part, after everyone was in bed, Martha and I would steal her brothers' bikes and take off down that dark rutted road. Only one house, the Zarubbas', was between our houses and the paved road. We were scared and felt so brave. It was fun.

The Zarubbas also had a lot of children, eight I believe, from the twenties down to nine. Virginia was in my class at school and would have been a pretty girl except she only had one perfect eye. I never knew what happened to the other, but it was disfigured. They were from Czechoslavakia, the parents, and really lived quite well. The mother was a little fat, foreign looking lady, always wore what looked like a dust cap and an apron—clean, clean, clean! They did not mingle with anyone that I knew of but me. I'm sure the older children had friends because they all had jobs and I thought they were good looking. I didn't go to see them often, but they would invite me for Sunday dinner some—again, a big, long table, plenty of food, a lot of talking, and always Jello or cake to finish. I felt a little strange, but since I knew I was welcome in a quiet way, I enjoyed being with them. Later when I was thirteen, John, probably twenty, started paying me a little attention, nothing much, but I knew. He had a pretty car, nice job, very good looking, Lawrence Olivier type. My mother knew he was looking because he would drive by for no reason, little things, really nothing to it, but that was the start of older boys for me. She should have explained to me that they were too old. I forgot to mention, Mr. Zarubba lived in Jacksonville, but they were not divorced because they were Catholic. I went to confession a time or two with Virginia, asked her what she said. What a confession—"Said bad words and cursed and sassed my mother." She really knew the bad words. I heard them. I admired her mother because she took such good care of her family. Sometimes I would be there when she was ironing. As she found a button off or a tear or a hole in a sock, she would hand it to Virginia to repair on the spot. I wished for a home like that.

I can't leave out Mrs. Case and her sister, Mrs. Smith. They were friends of my mother even though they were much older. We could always borrow a cup of sugar or a loaf of bread from them, plus, since my mother was deadly afraid of the fierce local thunderstorms, we would go to their house when a bad one came up. We kids sort of liked to go see these ladies. We made fun of them behind their backs because they were not attractive at all. Fat, both of them, and Mrs. Case did not wear her teeth and she also smoked. But she had a Victrola, that magic box, and she would play it with great pleasure. She was really very kind.

Melbourne actually was made up of three parts, the well-to-do and middle class, Melbourne Beach where some year-round folks lived and people from the north who came down for the winter, and people like us. Looking back, I suppose we were the poorest family in town. I'm sure we were on welfare even though it was never mentioned. I know the younger children got breakfast and lunch at school through some kind of program.

We had a good school, three nice buildings, a small football field, basketball court, good school spirit. I would have been much happier if books had been furnished. We bought them second hand when we could. But most of the time we only had one or two and, in order to study, I had to get to school early and borrow someone else's books. That was a hard way to get an education. We never had enough paper or pencils, always had to borrow a sheet of paper from the person sitting near, which was very uncomfortable for a child.

We had no clothes except hand-me-downs that my grandmother got from her stepchildren. Of course, they didn't fit. I remember one green dressy dress with some kind of braid trim, a terrible dress. I knew it was awful but told myself, "If you wear this hideous thing long enough, it will finally look good on you." Even though I was tacky looking and so poor, I still had friends. Melbourne, like many small towns, only had one school. So, we were all thrown together. Lucky for me, the girls from the best families were in my class and were friendly.

Virginia Edwards' father owned the only drug store in town. She had an older sister, Tracy, and lived in a pretty house by the river. She and her sister were so good looking, most popular girls. Someone made a lot of their clothes. I remember one jumper that crossed in the back made of light blue pique and Virginia wore a crisp, short sleeved white shirt with it. And I knew I would die for that jumper. I was in her room once while her sister was trying on clothes. Their room was enormous with two beds covered with clothes. I simply could not believe it. They were fun and kind to me. I don't believe that they were showing off. One time Virginia and I were going someplace and her mother was driving us. She turned to Virginia and asked her if she had brushed her teeth. She hadn't, so back to their house we went. While Virginia went in to brush her teeth, her mother asked me if my mother ever had to remind me to brush my teeth. I don't remember my answer but it was probably yes because I did have good manners, but I didn't even have a toothbrush and my mother was too busy worrying about food, much less teeth. Those were the times when I wished for good, caring parents.

Marilyn Tubbs' father was older and was the wealthiest man in Melbourne. Marilyn was adorable, a pretty blond with a great figure, smart, agreeable, and not conceited that I could tell. She invited me to her house after school some. She knew someone who had a canoe and lived on a little pond. So, one Saturday morning she taught me to paddle a canoe. What a wonderful life she had. I had dinner one night with them, I believe before a Girl Scout meeting, and her mother asked me if I liked beef tongue. I'd never heard of it, but it was food and I liked it. They had a cook/housekeeper who they called "Cook," a yard man, two cars, a big brick house with a mammoth brick flower pot built in their side yard. Also, a telephone! Once Marilyn broke her leg and was out of school for a while. Her mother invited the entire class over for angel food cake. I couldn't believe such wealth. There was Marilyn propped up in a beautiful bed in her own room.

Sadie Sloan was also quite rich. Her father was a bootlegger and resided in the Atlanta Penitentiary at that time. I believe he did get out before we left Melbourne. Sadie was another pretty blond girl who had a new convertible even though she was only twelve years old. Back then, if you had a car, you could drive it, no matter what age. Sadie was old beyond her years, very quiet, perhaps because her father was in the penitentiary, but friendly in her way. She was not out to impress anyone. She simply had this great car, wonderful clothes, a beautiful home, just a bit sad I thought. What was I doing thinking at that age? They had had a tragedy earlier. Sadie had two younger sisters. And one, while still a baby, maybe three years old, was left with the maid and, while dancing around a candle, caught fire and died. Well, the whole family never got over that. She also had an older brother who seemed sullen to me, but probably felt the responsibility of the family since he was the only boy and was around eighteen years old. They had a bulldog—and you can believe this or not—but the rumor was that Don, the brother, fed the dog buckshot to make him mean. I visited Sadie a few times but we were not real close. I know I was very young when I went to see her after school and we spent a lot of time in a regular playroom, a big blackboard and all sorts of interesting things. But somehow I felt sad for them.

Then there was Kitty Lattimer. She was probably not special to many folks, but I liked Kitty. Her parents were the best of all. Another large family, seven or eight children. Kitty's father owned the Melbourne Times. Their oldest daughter got pregnant, and never did marry the fellow. She had the baby and continued to live with her parents. That should have taught me something about good parents, very unselfish. Mr. Lattimer always had a little thing he did when he kissed his wife goodbye usually at the noontime meal. Mr. Lattimer always looked tired to me, but he was a good provider and father, not too great looking, but loved his wife who was a pretty woman with dark hair drawn up on the top of her head. We thought all parents were old then, but even though they had children up to twenty years old, I believe they were at least young at heart. Kitty and I were pretty good friends and she was fairly popular with the kids at school, a good all-round sport. Incidentally, I had some fine meals at their house also.

My thirteenth year was a bit confusing. Before that Martha V.L. found out about a strawberry farm that was sending a truck in every day to gather workers to pick strawberries. Martha was two years older than I was and always knew about people and things. Well, the next thing you knew I was on that truck before dawn one morning going to pick strawberries. It wasn't too bad, just hot and no place to go to the bathroom. (I found out later there was a little portable.) Anyway, these folks that were in charge of the pickers were young men from Russia, who, even though they'd been in the USA for a while, still spoke with an accent. Two of them and a girl ran the help for the farm. That was not a good place for young girls to be.

My first boyfriend was John J. Fields. He was a buck toothed, blond boy from Eau Gallie, a little town about thirteen miles from Melbourne. This boy never came in our house, just drove his truck, a great big one, and we would ride and he would sing. I liked that he had a pretty good voice. It seems to me that my mother never met him. Our schools were great football rivals, we both had good teams. John J's brother, Sam, was on the first-string team and John J. got to play also, but he was younger. Nothing much to that little romance. He was just a nice boy, I liked him. We didn't really date so much as just walk around together.

My mother and stepfather had never gotten along since moving to Melbourne, but they kept on having children and miscarriages. One was especially bad, too bad to write about. It left a lasting impression on me and, I'm sure, my older brother.

A peach warehouse opened up in Melbourne right on the main street. Martha and I would go out and get culls. Somehow we met a couple of truck drivers, very young, but far older than we were. One nice boy seemed to like me and wanted to see me. I shudder to think what could have happened to me. There again, my mother let me see him. I cannot believe anyone could be interested in a thirteen-year-old girl. He turned out to be so nice, just someone who wanted to sing to me. He had a truck route from Jacksonville to Melbourne. And when my mother found out about that, her wheels started turning. She must have had thoughts about going to Atlanta. So, she thought that if Bill, my oldest brother, and I could get a ride as far as Jacksonville, that would help. I could not get up the courage to ask this young man to take us, but I didn't tell her. One morning she set out walking with four small children. Hal, my brother, was the oldest of that crew and he was ten. She really didn't know what was going to happen to Bill and me except she hoped we would get a ride as far as Jacksonville. Then what? No plans, we were on our own, Bill was fifteen and a half and I was thirteen and a half. Someone saw her on the highway (she had gotten about ten miles) and ran back and told my stepfather that his family was hitchhiking along the road. He got them and brought them back home. So, Bill and I were scared. I really didn't know what we were going to do, we were abandoned.

My mother was serious and would not stay in Melbourne. So he gave her his beat up, one-seated car to go to Atlanta. So, that's the way we went to Atlanta and my entire life was turned around for the better. It's too bad the rest of them had to return because she was pregnant. They had three more years of terrible times. Bill left home to bum around the USA, June went to live with Marda. That left Hal, John and Margaret.

At Melbourne High School we were taught by Mrs. Bliss. She was truly misnamed, a little grey headed lady who spent little time being pleasant to students. Funny how one conversation stands out in my mind. On the first day of school we each had to stand and tell our name and tell where we were from. Very few were from Melbourne, since a lot of folks had moved there during the Florida boom. Well, one boy stood up and said he was from North Carlina. He was just a good old southern boy and that's the way he talked. But Mrs. Bliss made a big thing out of it, "It should have been pronounced North Carolina and don't forget it!"

Our school buildings were modern, extremely well equipped, I suppose because they were built during the Florida boom and there was plenty of money and a promise of more that did not materialize. Our playgrounds were most spacious, with swing sets and slides behind the middle and lower school building. We had several areas for sports activities, football, baseball and basketball, also plenty of room for spectators since we played out of town schools. Our school spirit was fabulous from first grade on, a big crowd turned out for all games. We also had a good band that any school would have been proud of. I loved to be walking past the school in late afternoons and to hear them practice and to hear children playing on the playground. Grammar school was easy because our books were furnished. So, consequently I made good grades. Reading was always my joy. And, since Melbourne had a well-equipped library, I never ran out of books.

At times when we lived close enough to our school to walk home for lunch, we did. But when we didn't, our lunches were different and we were a bit self-conscious when we were around our friends. The sandwich I most remember was a pork and bean sandwich. Our poor mother was not a good cook or homemaker, partly because she grew up as an only child and was neglectfully spoiled and partly because she had nothing or very little to cook or to cook with. However, at times she would make a big effort and, even though bread was only a nickel a loaf, she would get the urge to make homemade bread.

We had no gas or electricity. So, all of the cooking was done on a kerosene stove of sorts, always rickety and always smelly with a little tin oven that had to be put on one of the two burners in order to bake. So, baking bread was quite an undertaking and invariably the bread was full of holes, so we had trouble keeping our beans from falling out. I remember feeling so poor and unhappy because I didn't have a bologna sandwich like the other kids that I would hide behind a big pine tree and eat my pork and bean sandwich. But I love pork and beans to this day!

# CHAPTER
# FOUR

## THE DEPRESSION

My life changed drastically during my fourteenth year. That's the year that I came back to Atlanta to live with my grandmother. Little did I realize that hers also changed, not so much because of me, but very likely because of the financial strain that our family, my mother and my five brothers and sisters, put on her.

We charged into Atlanta one afternoon in March of 1931 in the most dilapidated, old, one-seated automobile, children of all ages spilling all over. We propped the trunk open with a big board so some of us could ride there. I was happy to choose the trunk because I could not endure my brother Bill and my mother smoking. Bill, the oldest at sixteen, did most of the driving and, I suppose, did very well since we arrived in one big messy piece right through the heart of Atlanta, Five Points. What a sight that must have been!

I believe we were expected. However, my mother was not limited to small surprises. More than likely she had sent a telegram the day before. Anyway, when we finally found my grandmother's big, really nice house up on a hill on Boulevard NE, our step aunts, Tommie and Betty, greeted us with open arms and most of all food. They were the most friendly and, I thought, the prettiest young women in the world. I had last seen them when I was around four years old. They were really charming, happy people, laughing, hugging us. We were certainly not used to that.

Gramma arrived around six that evening, helping my step-grandfather get around. He had Parkinson's' disease plus palsy or something, though still a very handsome man, goatee and all. He too I remembered from my baby years kindly. Gramma's hit and run accident several years earlier had left her with one leg shorter than the other and a bad limp, as well as being blind in one eye. So, there we were, a seedy, bewildered family of six kids and a young mother, thirty-six years old, piling in on an older crippled couple and we were made to feel so welcome. My grandmother was really not so old, perhaps fifty-five or so, still a lovely intelligent lady with beautiful manners.

Her household was already busy with people. The house had plenty of space; large living areas plus the master bedroom downstairs, and perhaps six bedrooms and a sleeping porch upstairs. Let me name the folks that already lived there besides Gramma and Doc. There was Gramma's sister, my Great Aunt Kit, always perfectly groomed, a genteel and stately lady, and Ken, Gramma and Kit's handsome twenty-four-year-old nephew, who'd been raised by Kit after his parents died. Ken had what we thought was a wonderful job at Hertz You Drive It in downtown Atlanta, drove a convertible, and danced like Fred Astaire. I fell in love at first sight. Tommie, single and personable, was one of Doc's six children. Her sister Betty was Doc's youngest and she, along with her husband Buck Buckaloo— I'm sure he had a name other than Buck but I never knew it—completed the five people who already lived there. And then came the seven of us. Gramma had a maid/cook named Mary who was a gem. Poor thing—how in the world could she cook and keep house for so many? Well, that was solved in about six weeks. My mother was pregnant again! She had left my stepfather in Melbourne, Florida because she could not stand him and discovered she had to go back.

Somehow it was decided that I should stay, perhaps because of my age plus I was getting interested in boys and they in me. I am sure I was a bit too independent, especially as far as my mother was

concerned, because I did not care for my stepfather and was beginning to lose my fear in letting them know it. So I stayed on with
my grandmother. That was when my life changed completely.

I was fourteen years old and happy to be leaving the nice clean
Florida area and moving to wonderful polluted Atlanta. I loved it.
The smells of the streetcars and burning leaves, the sound of sirens,
the newsboys yelling "Extra." It didn't have to be big news, they just
liked to yell to sell papers.

I'm sure things were bad—the economy was at rock bottom—
but my life was so different. I thought I had come to the promised
land. There was plenty of food. My new family, Gramma, Doc, Ken
and dear old Aunt Kit were all loving and pleasant. No one argued,
no yelling, just nice, civilized living.

Even though life was easier (it was like I was an only child now),
I was pretty mixed up and homesick for my brothers and sisters;
after all, some were just babies and I had been the one to care for
them most of the time.

Looking back, I can see my grandmother's life crumble maybe
because of that one move. She thought we were all there to stay.
What she was going to do with us even she didn't know, but she was
devoted to my mother and also was a very religious woman, Seventh
Day Adventist.

The die was already set. Even though my mother had to return
to Melbourne (she really must have been unhappy), my grandmother's
family of boarders, seeing a crowded, hopeless situation, had each
decided to move. My Aunt Kit had a home in Ravenna, Ohio, so
she went back. Betty and Buck moved into an apartment, and so
did Tommie. So, that left only Ken and me. Even though Gramma
was a brilliant woman and had always made a good living, I suppose
things really got tough financially so we moved a few months later
to a rented house in Buckhead on Brookwood Drive off of Lindberg
Drive.

I entered North Fulton High School where most of the prominent people sent their children and soon I had plenty of friends. I
went to the Seventh Day Adventist church on Saturday with my
grandmother, and on Sunday nights to the Presbyterian Church on

Peachtree Street with my friends. Life was indeed different, but good. Even though Ken was ten years older than I was, he was very good to me and I got to see a bit more of Atlanta than I ordinarily would have.

Every afternoon, the radio would broadcast the dance marathon that was going on at Palais Peachtree, a sort of dance hall or auditorium. These crazy people would see how long they could move around before they passed out or went to sleep. Red Skelton hosted the broadcast, and I found it interesting. I never entered a dance marathon but I did go to the Rollerdome with Ken where we would skate to music.

The musicals in theaters were beautiful by then; Nelson Eddy and Jeanette McDonald, Bing Crosby, the newly-discovered Frank Sinatra, Fred Astaire and Ginger Rogers, George Burns. By the time I was sixteen, Aunt Kit had moved back in with us. And since she loved movies, especially musicals, she and I would ride the streetcar downtown and have a wonderful time.

I had plenty of boyfriends. None of them had any money, but that didn't matter. A date then meant a walk in the park and maybe a cherry Coke at the corner drugstore. I remember they had dances on Friday nights in the park. I went to these some. They were fun and harmless. Everything was harmless back then. At sixteen, I could ride the streetcar at night, and feel perfectly safe.

I soon met a wonderful girl who lived on Lindberg Drive in the most beautiful house on that street. Her name was Jean Chapman, and her father was a prominent architect in Atlanta. She was sometimes unhappy, mainly because her parents didn't get along. I remember her playing piano, such lovely tunes, one of her favorites being "Some Day My Prince Will Come." Well, he did. She was only sixteen but they fell in love, eloped, and were married. I never heard from her again, but I'll always remember the good times at her house, particularly one big party, which the Townsend Brothers of bicycle-racing fame helped her put on. Some party!

We only lived on Brookwood Drive for about two years, during which time my grandmother's office was in the Grand Theater Building on the sixth floor in downtown Atlanta where it had been since probably before I was born. Well, maybe times got worse or maybe her office was too far from home, but we moved to Grant Park, which was a real come down. The first house was nice. But Gramma got the idea that if she moved into a duplex, then she could have her office on one side and our house on the other. So we moved two doors down on the corner of Boulevard SE and Berne St. It turned out to be a good move, right across from the entrance to Grant Park on the streetcar line.

My mother and brothers and sisters lived in Melbourne, Florida for about two years longer. I went down to visit one time when my stepfather's grown son, Homer, invited me to go with him and another couple when they were going to Cocoa Beach. Gramma gave me money for meals, which my mother promptly borrowed. When I started to leave for Atlanta, I asked for it back, but my stepfather told me that Homer had it. Later I found out, of course, that he didn't. So, being a stubborn child, I refused to eat all the way home. What a brat! I was so embarrassed and mad about the whole thing.

Sometime during those two years my sister, June, who was only six or seven, went to live with Marda and Harry Cain in Chicago. Marda was Doc's oldest daughter and oldest living child after the death of Baxter some years back. June apparently had a good life with Marda. Harry was a doctor and had a clinic with another doctor.

About the time that June left, my brother Bill left also. I never knew much about that until one day when I was home alone, the doorbell rang and a young hobo was at the door. Honestly I did not recognize him for a moment. But it was Bill. He had been riding the boxcars for perhaps a year. What a sight he was, it broke my heart. I really did not know what a hopeless plight he was in. My first act was to get him out of those rags and put them in a pot on the stove to boil. His shoes were ragged, he was very dirty, what a mess. Hungry also. He stayed with us for a while, then I believe he went back to Melbourne. All of this happened when we lived on Brookwood Drive. Eventually Bill too went to live with Marda and Harry in Chicago. Years later my sister June moved to Atlanta to work at the Rialto Theater selling tickets.

Perhaps the move to Grant Park was because we needed more room since Aunt Kit was coming back to live with us. Even though we moved into a rental house, Gramma had a little room and bath added to the back for a bedroom. She and Doc had that, Aunt Kit had a room off of the kitchen which was originally the dining room, Ken had the sleeping porch, and I had the couch in a back room of my grandmother's office/clinic. This house was a nice duplex on a corner lot with a large porch. We all came to like being there. Aunt Kit was a real dear. She had a good sense of humor, played Solitaire and rummy at all times. She got up in the morning, dressed neatly, put on her pearls and was ready for the day. I played cards with her most every day, and manicured her nails. She and I got along fine. I loved hearing her talk about her girlfriends, to all of whom she wrote letters as long as they lived. They all lived in Cleveland, Toledo or Ravenna, Ohio. Aunt Kit was really not so old then, I guess in her seventies. The most exercise she ever took was pushing those playing cards around. Looking back, when I first came to Atlanta she did get around more. She and I rode the streetcar to Sears on Ponce de Leon once and she bought me a pair of shoes. I had never seen a store that large. I remember that day well. One time we went downtown to Rich's mainly for lunch, I believe. Aunt Kit loved to have creamed chicken on cornbread. Another time, several times actually, we went to a movie downtown. She thought Fred Astaire was wonderful and so did I. Then we went to an ice cream sundae place a little down from Loew's Grand Theater. Aunt Kit had a very meager amount to live on but since she had always lived quite well, she managed it with a flair. She never complained, always pleasant, so elegant, but not stiff. In her younger years she had always worked in an office until she finally married Jim Newman who lived in back of her and was quite well to do. She married him after his wife died and Aunt Kit was fifty years old. When we heard that, we thought she was really old. Little did we know! They spent their winters in St. Augustine and their summers in Ravenna. I never met him but she thought he was wonderful and told me all about him. She lived to be ninety-seven.

I had lived in Atlanta for about two years when my mother and the rest of the children decided to move again. It seems to me that my stepfather came also. He and my mother lived together off and on until he died. During part of that time when they were not together, the rest of the family moved into a house on Killian Street just a street over from us in Grant Park. Most of these houses were two family dwellings. They lived on the first floor.

My mother made a lot of mistakes, mostly marrying the wrong men, but she was not lazy. She was forever thinking up ways to make money. I remember in Melbourne she put us little kids up to selling Bibles, and then some kind of fluffy cheese chips. Of course, we didn't sell any Bibles and we ended up eating all of the cheese chips. After moving to Atlanta, she was desperate, with children to feed and a husband who was around some but never contributed in any way but to make babies. She decided to open a small laundry in her home. That meant buying equipment. Washing machines were not much in those days—hoses running in and out and separate wringers, some of which had to be cranked by hand. Dryers weren't around yet, so clothes lines were used outside. An ironer called the mangle was the most help. You could iron all flat ware, shirts and pants or anything else if you were adept at it. That wasn't too bad of an undertaking. She hired one or two women to help, so it held up for a while. How she got the order from the Frances Virginia Tearoom in downtown, I don't know, but she did. That was "the" tearoom. Everyone went there and loved it.

She found out that they were enlarging and adding a salad bar, so suggested that I apply for a counter girl job, which I did and got it. I was nearly seventeen then and had never worked except to help my grandmother get out letters and to keep the office rooms clean, also to clean our part of the house, those kinds of things. In those days we had grate fires of coal that had to be banked with ashes at night and then started again the next morning. Some rooms had gas heaters, especially in the office.

Before I got the job at the Tearoom my grandmother had an automobile accident. She and Doc were both hurt. She had, among other injuries, a broken collar bone and poor Doc was bunged up which just added to his miseries. That was a hard time for them. I had to do for all of them. Aunt Kit was never able to do much. She had rheumatism and had to have a good rub down every night. I got pretty good at that. So, my schedule was pretty full. It is too bad I couldn't drive. Anyway, I managed to keep everyone happy, even helped Gramma with her patients. She taught me to give a passable massage to her female patients. She called Ken in for adjustments since he was a chiropractor, or at least had a certificate. She called him Dr. Searl, his last name, and no one seemed to know the difference. I know he was glad when that was over. I was able to stay out until ten o'clock each night, then it was time to tuck everyone in, give the rub downs, put Doc's feet in bed—he could sit on the bed but then it was up to someone else to get the rest of him in, but he was very helpful. Gramma was in the most pain plus when her collar bone started to heal it itched under the cast. So, I learned to poke around with powder and stuff and make her comfortable. She did a lot and never called me at night even to help with Doc. It wasn't so bad, we had a pretty good system and everyone worked at it.

# CHAPTER
# FIVE

## WESLEY

Since I was thirteen I'd had boyfriends, but everyone did, that was the way it was. I suppose some girls went steady, but I didn't. I always had three or four boys that I went out with or just saw. I was used to boys coming on to me and paying me a lot of attention but had not felt anything but fun for any of them—well, maybe a little for one older fellow who'd been a high school teacher and athletic coach at a small school. When I met him he was looking for another job. His name was Charlie Roberts and I had met him through his sister, Isabel, who I knew from a millinery class. I did like Charlie but he was ten years older than I was and had a serious girlfriend who was in college someplace other than Atlanta. Anyway, even though we had fun together, he never led me on. He very soon got a job as a high school sports writer for the Atlanta Constitution and after a few years married the girl that he was waiting for. Keep in mind, I was only sixteen years old and, like most sixteen-year-olds, I was sure I knew enough to take care of myself. As it turned out, I really did. With a little luck thrown in.

So there was nothing serious until a fellow, just a friend, brought a young man by to see me on a Sunday night. And that did it! I thought he was the handsomest, cutest, smartest, just the one for me kind of fellow I had ever met. I remember he had a lot of blond curly hair and wore a black overcoat. So good looking. Well, he felt the same for me, asked me out for the next Saturday night but all seventeen years of my life said no, I was busy. I wasn't but knew I would be if I wanted and I was saving Saturday night. He asked about Tuesday night and I said yes, and after that, the rest of his life.

Wesley Paris was his name and he told me I was going to marry him on that first Tuesday date, and went home and told his mother and sisters that he had met the girl he was going to marry. He was the only boy in the family. His father had a job in Virginia Beach in a shipyard, apparently had been there for years, a good job but his family never moved there. Wesley was smart. Upon graduating from Commercial High School he went with a steamship line, doing some office work and typing. He was a fast typist. After a few months he went with Cotton Producers Association in the fertilizer department located in the 101 Building on Marietta Street. His boss was Ed S. Cook who worked under D.W. Brooks, the founder of the great-to-be Farmers' Cooperative. Mr. Brooks had formed that small company with just three men and a boy, Wesley being the boy. Wesley loved the job and felt that he had a great future there. How sweet life was! I had the smartest, most wonderful person on earth and he thought I was right for him. We were in love.

Then in a few months his father came home sick. He had advanced colon cancer. Shortly after we made our first mistake, we eloped. The entire world came down on us. Looking back, we were wrong. He was making eighty dollars a month and his family depended on his salary and that of his sister.

We were going to keep our marriage a secret, as some of our friends did. Elopement was not uncommon in those days. There was no money for weddings. In my case no one really cared, they just put up a fuss, I suppose, because they weren't in on it. They should have known. Wesley had given me a ring several months before. He really meant business.

We knew that we wanted to be together and be married. Back

then there was no such thing as living together. For one thing, there was no birth control available. We knew nothing. The mistake was we eloped one Sunday morning—it was June 16, 1935—on the way to a BYPU retreat for the day. We decided a few days ahead but told no one. Our friends Bob Bishop and Ruth Thomas were to pick us up in Ruth's one-seated car (she could not drive), which they did. When we told them to stop in Marietta at the Justice of the Peace's house, they could not believe us. However, they stopped. Since it was early Sunday morning, we took the Justice of the Peace a bit by surprise; he hadn't showered or dressed. So we had to wait a while. His wife was sweet and, since I did not have a flower, picked some gardenias and pinned them on us. I am sure they could not understand why in the world we decided to marry so early in the morning. I looked young, even for eighteen. But after questioning us—and when Bob and Ruth swore that I was old enough—they went ahead with the short ceremony. Back then you had no identification, no Social Security number or driver's license. We would not have had a license anyway; we had no car and neither of us could drive.

Getting married was not all fun because we had feelings of responsibility. Wesley was giving most of what he made to his family and I was only making seven dollars a week, of which I gave five to my mother. (Incidentally, the Frances Virginia Tearoom also gave me two delicious meals a day.) I really kept very little except car fare for myself. But those were hard times and my mother had small children and no husband, so that had to be done. Besides, she was the one who told me about the job.

We had planned to elope several weeks ahead and I did want a new dress. Looking back, that was pretty sad because I only had the barest necessities, perhaps only two or maybe three dresses. I did have a bright green coat that I had bought on layaway at High's Department Store on Whitehall Street, which was a continuation of Peachtree Street. Because folks seemed to notice me more, I often wondered if the coat was too green. Now I realize that I was growing up and with my red hair and freckles the coat made me pretty. I bought a brown dress that I liked a lot. It had full, thin sleeves and was quite long, as was the style then. There again, I bought it on layaway and probably did not pay for it until long after we were married. The dress probably cost eighteen dollars.

Since I had not told anyone of our plans, we were able to keep our marriage a secret for one week. Then Wesley decided, "To heck with that." He was only nineteen, but, as was my nature then, I listened to everything he said and truly believed it was true. We had other friends a little older than we were who were married and had a car. Somehow Wesley arranged with them to take us on an overnight trip. They were attractive, fun people who Wesley had grown up with. Even though he knew them better than I did, it worked fine. If we had not been feeling so guilty and absolutely scared to death, we would have had a good time. We went to a well-known fishing camp in north Georgia. We didn't fish but did go boating in a little row boat.

Of course, we had to tell our folks. So, on the way, we stopped to send a telegram to each family. I cannot believe how foolish we were! We couldn't leave until I had finished work at about eight o'clock on Saturday night. Something made me think I had better not just disappear. Even though I was young, I still had a strong sense of responsibility and I did love my grandmother and my family. I did care what they thought and certainly did not want to worry them. Actually the problem was not with my family but with Wesley's. My folks might have—would have—had plenty to say about my getting married, not that they could see anything else in store for me. We were all so poor. But times had been better for my grandmother and Aunt Kit, so they very likely had hope for me.

This was a big step for me. Had I been a few years older, I would never have done it. I know that now. I had met Wesley's family but that was about all, was not impressed in the least. His mother was not attractive and the side of her that I saw was not especially kind. This is all leading up to the uncertainty of what I was about to do. Love and youth are some kind of a blind combination, but it meant nothing to us. Wesley and I were also a combination. We felt able to conquer the little part of the world we occupied.

I was not thinking too far ahead, simply going along for the most part with what Wesley had in mind. He was a smart boy and very persuasive, so I went along with whatever he planned. All he knew was that he was not going to be married and have to wait indefinitely to get things moving. I had not thought far enough ahead, not past our little one night and one day trip to someplace in north Georgia—it turned out to be Platt's Fishing Camp—that our friends Doris and Robert Preston knew about. It was rustic but right on the lake and very pretty and quite comfortable. Like the Justice of the Peace and his wife, the folks that ran the camp questioned my age. I must have looked fifteen. Doris and Robert had been married a few years and were a little older. So, they assured these folks that I was really eighteen and also we had a marriage license. Thus began a long and, for the most part, happy marriage bound by a lasting love. I loved and still do, even though Wesley died in 1972. I'll always remember hearing music coming across the lake that night. Someone—I wonder if it was the owner of the camp—must have had a Victrola, because they played one record over and over again; "Every night I fall in love all over again with you."

On returning from our wedding trip we immediately went to Wesley's house to face the music. We knew it would be bad, Wesley more than I because he knew his family. Well, they really did break loose! I can see their side now but it truly was a sad awakening for me there. His father was sick with no hope for living more than a year. They were left with no income since he was working by the job. That left Wesley and his sister, Mabel, to support the family. They both had jobs but I am sure they thought Wesley would desert them. So, of course, they hated me, and for good reason. Wesley had no intention of leaving. But since we had not discussed what was going to happen, I really did not know. That was the beginning of me learning to depend on another person to make decisions concerning me. Though I suppose that had been going on all of my life since I had not really made it to adulthood by the time I married. I learned by bits and pieces along the way to rely upon myself. The hard way, I might add.

Mabel was older than Wesley by about two years and his other sister, Elsie, was younger by two. Mabel was different from most girls in that she had no interest in boys or, by that time, men. Nor did she pay attention to her appearance. She was clean and neat but it stopped there. She was not attractive looking or acting, had a shrill voice, and was the boss of that family. All in all she was not about to be pleasant. She loved her brother, but when he married she turned on him with a fury from hell. Needless to say, she hated me. I was about as miserable as a person could be, exchanging my good, genteel grandmother, my Aunt Kit and Cousin Ken for these hateful people that seemed to have come from another world. Both sisters, like Wesley, were smart, but I don't know how that happened because the parents were uneducated, the mother fat with bad teeth damaged from a lifetime of dipping snuff. I did not know the father very well and apparently they didn't either because he worked in other cities most of the time. He was a sheet metal worker and must have made a fair living—no doubt a good man because from what I could gather he sent most of his wages home to support his family. When he stopped working, the money stopped.

Wesley and I ended up sleeping in their dining room, buying some bedroom furniture at a department store named Highs. That was pretty rugged because those little houses were built straight back, one room in back of another. To make matters worse, they lived in a duplex with one bathroom. Since the dining room was in the middle it made for awkward living, even though we could shut the doors leading to his father's sick room and on the other end to the kitchen. We had little privacy. Noises from each of the other rooms were just like there were no separations and it went both ways, they could hear everything that went on in our room. I remember one time Wesley was tickling me—and that did happen even though we were miserable—Mabel called out, "Quiet down in there."

Streetcars had front and back doors. If Mabel was on the same car, she would exit via whichever door I did not use even though we were going into the same house. It took a while to get used to that, but get used to it I did.

I continued working at the Frances Virginia Tearoom, riding the streetcar, which was handy because even though I had to transfer downtown it stopped right in front of their house. In those days a young woman was perfectly safe being out at night. And since I was home by nine or nine-thirty, that worked out fine. I remember sitting by the window in the streetcar and seeing my reflection thinking, "What has a pretty girl like you come to?" Even though I was in love, I still wondered.

Then the climax came. We thought I was pregnant by the second month of our marriage. Keep in mind, birth control was unknown, other than a little protection by the husband. After a few anxious days we found out not. In spite of the relief, I believe we—especially Wesley—were a little disappointed. So, as usual, I (dumb bunny) listened and did get pregnant. He had unhappiness on both sides, a very unhappy wife and family.

We lived there for about five months. Then under pressure from me, he said if I could find a place for us to live for ten dollars a month we would move. At that time he was making a hundred dollars a month and giving his mother eighty. Of course, by that time I had to quit working, which didn't make any difference anyway since I was still giving my mother five dollars out of my seven dollars. When she found out I was expecting a baby, true to her past performances, she started thrashing around and crying, "Oh, I am taking blood money." What dramatics! But that could be expected. I remember my grandmother saying, knowing full well that we didn't have any money, "If Wesley is supporting his family, you should certainly give your mother her due." I always thought she was fair, but that was a bit hard to take since my brother, Bill (two years older than I was and unemployed) drove my mother's car, smoking a cigarette, to meet me on pay day to pick up my money. Life was confusing. I really believe Wesley had all of this figured out. He would have loved to have supported me and made enough to do so except that his family had to have it, which I certainly understood.

I found a place to live! It was advertised in the newspaper. It was the year of the big snow and ice storm, 1935, so I put on my boots and walked through about ten inches of treacherous snow and ice, to apply in person. I don't know how far I walked, but I would say around two miles. On the way I met some boys that I knew and, of course, they threw snowballs. I don't believe they knew I was married, much less pregnant.

Mrs. Arnold, who had the rooms for rent, had said "No Children" in her advertisement, so I kept my coat on when we talked. I hadn't fooled her but, being the kind woman that she was, she never let me know that she knew until after we had moved in. She knew I was desperate, I guess. And she was right; I would have done anything to get those rooms.

We had two back rooms sharing a bathroom heated only for baths by a little kerosene heater. We had a large sink and a coal stove in our kitchen. Believe me, we were in heaven. Mrs. Arnold and her husband and fifteen-year-old beautiful, spoiled, delightful daughter lived in the rest of the rental house.

That was the hardest time because of very tight money but the best of times otherwise since that was the beginning of everyone relaxing a bit. Wesley's family was as glad to have us move as we were to move. Wesley asked Mr. Brooks for a raise and received twenty-five dollars more per month.

We were still paying for our bedroom furniture but had to have some kitchen things, a small range and table and four chairs. The refrigerator had to wait. However, since that was a cold winter, we put food on the back porch and managed for a few months. We were able to buy a little four-foot Kenmore before summer and the baby arrived.

Those were happy days. We could be alone. Wesley was a hard worker from the very beginning and never changed. So, I was by myself much of the time. Mrs. Arnold and her daughter, Dorothy, were company for me. (Dorothy and I have remained friends. We went to Ireland together in 1995 on a University of Georgia tour and had a wonderful time. Isn't it nice to remain friends all of these years? She has to be the spiciest, brightest woman around. She taught sociology in a southern California college for years and has had a text book published on Elvis.)

Life was good again even though Wesley was very sorry that his father was dying and did die before our baby was born.

Elaine was our first child. She arrived one month late on June 2nd, 1936, a beautiful baby born to two children who thought they were grown at eighteen and nineteen. She cried for one month, I suppose hoping we would send her back. Who knows why? All I know is we walked her most of every night. She may have been hungry. We had one doctor, a very well-known one. Looking back, we should have had an OB/GYN and a pediatrician, but that would have been hard because of our money problems. Those were the days of no insurance except life insurance. We continued to live in the Arnolds' house for about one year. During that time Wesley's father died. Wes, of course, kept on with his part of his mother's and Elsie's expenses. However, tempers smoothed over. So, life was still poor but much easier. We got used to having a baby to care for and she, Elaine, got used to us.

Wesley worked days and most nights until nearly midnight, me always thinking it was a temporary thing. But little did I know, that was a way of life. He was determined to make something of himself, he enjoyed doing it and over the years it paid off. I really didn't know anything else. Times were different then. There was no way for me to work out of the home. Jobs were simply not available, anyway those of any substance. I'm not sure today's women have it so much better. They usually work, then come home to do dinner, tend children and housework. They have a certain amount of independence that we didn't have in those days. However, it seems to all even out. I've had to become independent because of the death of my husband. And, believe me, it was hard. Even though life was somewhat different in my younger days, after the first few hard years our lives were much easier. Money was not a problem because Wesley, true to his word, made it in his career. He reached the top of Gold Kist (Cotton Producers) and was most generous with me. We traveled all over the world, he just didn't live long enough, being only fifty-six when he died.

I'm rambling, so back to the story. We moved from the Arnolds' to a pretty duplex in east Atlanta on Florida Avenue. I loved being there and so did Wesley. After about two years the house was sold and we moved to an apartment closer to the city. Apartment life just wasn't for me. I didn't know anyone and had moved away from my friends. So, after perhaps a year we moved to a duplex on Oakland Avenue. It was pretty nice but old and had rats—and I mean grown rats! Elsie had given Elaine a baby duck for Easter but a tragic thing happened. We got up one morning and found its beak. I was baffled but not Wesley. I guess he knew about rats because we moved again in a hurry. He said if a rat was large enough to eat a baby duck, it might just hurt Elaine. Scary!

From there we moved to a house off of Moreland Avenue. I was pregnant with Anita by then and those were pretty happy years. Wesley was making more money and we had our good friends, Bob and Ruth Bishop, to chum around with. We played Rook (a card game) almost every night and always ended up ordering hamburgers from a place called Two Points. We had fun and Elaine stayed up as long as we did. Sometimes I put her to bed. But she wasn't ready as a rule and I gave in. She and I slept late, so we had our own schedule. We listened to soap operas during the day. I'm sure that's why she likes them now. Of course, there was no TV then but radio was fun and that's all we knew.

Anita was such a pretty baby and a good one until she was two and then she was a handful. Even though we thought we knew babies by then, I'm afraid we didn't. Now I know what happens when children turn two, but didn't then.

We made one more move before we bought our first home. I learned to drive. We had a car by then. I'll never forget Wesley learning. First he bought a car. But since he couldn't drive, a woman from the dealership drove it home for him. He loaded Elaine and me into that car and we rode until late that night. He learned to drive with us in the car. That has to say something for youth. We were not afraid. Before we stopped we drove right through Five Points in the middle of Atlanta. In those days, there were no driver's licenses. If you had a car, you drove it.

Sometime later he decided—or I decided or maybe it just happened—that I should learn too. That's not all; Wesley taught me. Poor man, it wasn't fun for him. I learned okay. But when I went out for a solo drive, I forgot how to stop. So, I just ran into a sewer. Cars were more complicated then. You had to release the clutch and manipulate the gas and all that hard stuff! It's a good thing I learned when I did because that car was not long for our family. We decided to buy a house and needed some money. So, we sold the car. Back to street cars again and walking.

The house we found and bought was located in east Atlanta on Clay Street. It was a pretty white house on a nice corner lot. It was on the street car line, or rather the car line ran by the side street right by our house, so that was good. The only inconvenience was that the school was at least two miles from us and I had to walk Elaine and finally Anita to school and back, a lot of walking. Sam was born while we lived in this house. And by the time Anita started school, I was pushing him in a stroller and half dragging Anita because she hated school. We lived through that somehow.

During that time money was tight. Wesley's mother had died and Mabel and Elsie were renting a room not far from us. We were all the family they had, so they didn't get far away. We were getting along pretty well by then and we needed more money and they needed a better place to live. So, they moved in with us. They each paid us twenty-five dollars per month and I cooked and cleaned house for all of us. Wesley was working hard, long hours, but then so was I. That fifty dollars did not come to me but was used to keep us all going to some extent. In the meantime we were getting in debt, what with doctor bills and clothes for the kids and the like. When we finally did take stock of our debts, it added up to a tremendous sum of thirteen hundred dollars. That is not much now, but then it was impossible to pay off. Mabel and Elsie lived with us for a year or so or maybe three years. It was hard living. We had no privacy and I resented having to wait on them and having them around all of the time. Elsie met Houston and married and moved. Mabel moved in with the Hills whom she did not know. But they became friends and after Mrs. Hill died, Ray and Mabel married. But that's another story, and all happened years later.

World War II broke out while we lived on Clay Street. I remember coming home from church, turning on the radio and hearing that Pearl Harbor had been bombed. Everyone remembers what they were doing and where they were on that Sunday morning. My brother, Hal, was eighteen and was the first man to enlist in Atlanta. He went into training and ended up as a paratrooper. The old story of blackouts, food rationing, war bonds, recycling, all of those things we know so well. All of those things were hard but, since everyone was doing the same thing and we were all patriotic and wanted to do our best, it was just a way of life.

# CHAPTER
# SIX

## FROM CLAY STREET TO PINE LAKE

Wesley worked day and night to get ahead. He thrived on it and that was his way for the rest of his life. He never neglected his duty to his family, and did his part and more to support his mother until her death about five years later. By that time we had two little girls. Funny how children can turn people around. I don't believe his mother and sisters liked me any better, but they knew in order to see the children they had to accept me because I came first with Wesley.

We just sort of marked time for a few years. We had been married about six years, lived in rental houses, duplexes, etc. When we decided to buy a house, we found one that we could manage financially on Clay Street. I believe by that time there was some talk of Wesley's sisters, Mabel and Elsie, moving in with us since they were renting one or two rooms in someone's house. They were not happy together and were spending a lot of time with us, plus we could use the board money if we bought a house. Not a good idea for me, but that is what happened. Times were tough.

We had bought a new red car of some sort, that was the mighty purchase. Then things were not moving along at Cotton Producers in Wesley's favor as fast as he thought they should be. So, when he was offered a job at Firestore, the largest tire store on 10<sup>th</sup> and Peachtree, he took it. That proved to be good and bad. It made Cotton Producers wake up and see that they had lost a very promising young man. Also, it was not a good move for us. Wesley seemed happy enough, but down deep he believed in Cotton Producers. However, he was a man of conviction and did not plan to be mistreated. Well, that lasted nine months. Cotton Producers offered him more money and really wanted him back and he wanted to go back, so it all ended well.

In a lot of ways that was a bad experience for me. My perfect husband was working with a whole new different kind of people, for the most part single. He was young, good looking, and personable, and had married before he had seen the world. Also, he had a pregnant wife, two children, and two sisters who fouled up his married life. At work, he had plenty of distractions, single men, a couple of single girls, people who liked to party. Of course, I couldn't party, I was tied down plenty! We had never been drinking people. So, this was new to him and, I dare say, attractive. Some of this happened before I became pregnant for the third time. I suppose there is a certain amount of wildness in all of us, some of us just couldn't break away and be wild. Those fellows at Firestone just did not appeal to me. They decided—and Wesley was with them—to get in a car and see how many states they could travel to in a certain number of days, drinking all the way. Needless to say, that caused trouble in our family.

We rode that period out, it didn't last too long, and then it was back to Cotton Producers and hard work. Mr. Brooks hired an older man named Julian Baker to work with Wesley. Now, talk about drinking! Julian would come to dinner and find after a few drinks that his teeth were in the way, so out they came and rested next to his plate. Julian was from Richmond, Virginia. He and his wife, Martha, adopted their son, Joe, and were really quite refined people. The only problem was his whiskey but, goodness, what a problem. They came to Atlanta and moved into a lovely section of Decatur.

He was a real Virginian and missed Richmond. Julian was probably pretty well washed up in more ways than one when Mr. Brooks hired him, but nobody was aware of it, especially him. Martha and I were thrown together at company functions and we visited back and forth some, but were never really good friends. She was older than I was, more experienced, had taught school, and never had children until adopting Joe. She looked on me as a know nothing child and in some ways she was absolutely right. I knew nothing but to stay home and look after children the best I could and from time to time cook and clean after Wesley's sisters. I suppose I felt like Cinderella at times. Wesley had a hard time with Julian for a few years until Julian decided that he had had it and Wesley became the boss. In the end Martha died of cancer and Julian married a woman also named Martha, a nice enough lady. Julian became ill. I don't remember what went wrong but his mind became feeble, along with his body, and he died.

On Clay Street we had managed to get pretty much in debt, not much by today's standards, but bad for 1941. We owed lots of people and, when war was declared, Wesley buckled down and made a budget to pay those bills off, writing all of the folks that we owed telling them what we planned to do and how much they would get each month. We did, too.

War does different things to different people, but one thing for sure, no one stays the same. As I said, my brother, Hal, was the first person to enlist in Atlanta. He was snapped up and, before we knew it, he was gone. He had joined the 32nd Division (Airborne). He was an amateur boxer before he enlisted and was in perfect shape, a feather weight, red-headed dynamo. Hal was married to Marie, but they had no children. So, he was the one they wanted and he wanted to go. He served through the entire war, was in every theater of war in Europe and jumped on D Day and was captured after landing in a tree. How terrible that must have been for him. We didn't hear from him for nine months after his capture. My card from the prison came first. So, I called everyone. We really thought he was dead. You can imagine how happy we all were, so relieved, yet we didn't know how he was or what condition he was in. Over the war period I had received some letters and a few pictures; the first one of a young man, strong, good looking, carefree, with a perfect physique in swim trunks on a California beach. He had the world by the tail and was ready to swing it. Perhaps a year and a half later, another picture showed him still as strong, a little heavier, bearded, and clearly not so young. The war, the battles, the killings, the pure terror he must have felt many times all showed in this still handsome, still determined, still brave, and perhaps still young, man. The war can be described by those pictures.

Hal came home looking pretty fit on the outside. His teeth were bad and he didn't feel comfortable sleeping in a bed. But he played his guitar and sang war songs. We were so happy to have him home. Marie would be worried because he would start the night sleeping in the bed but by morning he would be on the floor, which he said he found more comfortable. Hal and Marie had a son, Mike, before Hal died of a massive heart attack at age 35.

My brother, John (the shy little nine-year-old he will always be to me), also enlisted when he became eighteen. He also became a paratrooper. That worried me. I could never imagine him jumping out of a plane, not that he wasn't brave enough, it probably took a lot more bravery on his part than the others because I know he must have been afraid. How can you be brave if you are never afraid? John was shot and sent home before the war ended. I believe the bullet was still lodged somewhere in his body long after the war, but it never stopped him from getting up to stuff!

The war kept on, bringing rationing, blackouts and all of that. Everyone did what they could. I still didn't work outside of our home even though some women worked in defense plants. I had three children and Mabel and Elsie living with us, so in a way I made a little money cooking and cleaning for them. We were really not spending one extra dime. For one thing, the war did not look good and they had gotten down to calling up men with children. So, we knew if things did not get better, Wesley would be called. He was. It wasn't that he was not patriotic. He was willing to go, but also he worried about us. The bills were still not paid and would not get paid now. But that was not too important. How in the world would I manage to live on the allotment sent me by the government? He left me $100 to start and was inducted into the Navy at Fort McPherson. I believe I was numb. More than likely I would have figured out a way to go to work to help support my children. I don't remember what was going through my mind. I think he had been at Fort McPherson for about a week when Mr. Brooks got him out for defense purposes. I couldn't believe it. He was sent to Savannah, Georgia to work in their fertilizer plant for the remainder of the war. He got to come home once every three months and I went to see him once during that period. I believe it lasted eighteen months. That was indeed better than war. I never even thought of complaining. I remember sitting at my desk at night writing him letters and crying my heart out. We all did a little growing up during that time.

Wesley did a little (or a lot) of everything at that plant. They had a man that managed it who had been there for a long time. I won't name him because he did something, it was rumored, that was not accepted at that time. He was supposed to be having an affair with a black woman. Black or white does not matter to me; in my mind, it's having an affair that is the wrong thing.

I remember the one time I went to see Wesley I rode the Nancy Hanks train all night. The woman I was sharing a seat with was so nice. She was older, maybe forty, and, of course, we talked. She had lovely diamond rings that I admired. I remember her words, "Your children are all diamonds." How true!

Those days ended with the war and things got back to normal, only better. The war at least brought an end to the Depression. What a strange way to end a depression! For your kids that think you can't possibly pay off large debts, this is the way we did it. We made out a list of everything we owed, I can still see it now, the yellow sheet. By each name we wrote the amount owed and also the amount we could pay each month. It took us eighteen months to get out of debt, but that taught us a good lesson. We have owed money since, but nothing that we couldn't handle.

We lived on Clay Street about seven years, during which time I painted all of the dark woodwork white, every room, a big job. We liked being in that house, especially since it was the first house we owned, having bought it for $3,100. We did not have washers or dryers or gas furnaces. I washed our clothes in a wash tub with a wash board and hung them out to dry on a clothes line. Most of the time I boiled them in soapy water on the stove.

We did have one luxury. We bought what was called a coal hopper. It was a huge tub like container that was filled with coal that was bought specially ground up for that purpose. We filled it with a big shovel about every three days. The hopper held five hundred pounds of coal. Since Wesley worked most of the time long hours and that time in Savannah, that left me to shovel the coal. I got pretty good at it even though I weighed less than a hundred pounds then. The bad thing about that hopper was sometimes clinkers would form and you had to remove them from the furnace with a big fork like thing. It was all run by an electric motor. Really quite an improvement over keeping a fire going with chunks of coal.

We were not rich, that is for sure. I remember our back steps. Two stairs about twenty steps up came loose from the house, and were very unsteady. But I kept going up and down them to hang out clothes and to bring them in. We couldn't afford to get them fixed and Wesley was not the handyman. So, he nailed the back door shut! Where there's a will, there's a way! That made me have to go out the front door and around the house. I really don't believe he knew the hardship of running a household without a husband around. These were hard days. I also remember when my two girls were old enough to start school—we lived two miles from the school—I had to push Sam, the baby, in his tailor-tot those miles in order to walk the girls to school. We finally got a car. It seemed our cars came and went during those days.

This was the thought back then: The man had the freedom of earning the living and that was that. Everything else was done by the woman. There was never a thought that a woman with children could go to work, just single girls like Mabel and Elsie. I didn't have the education or the courage to do otherwise, but I would not do that again. I would find a way out. It paid off later but for a while I was going down the wrong track. Probably what bothers me most now was the lack of privacy that we had; there was always someone else in that small house, demanding Wesley's attention and that of my children. We didn't feel free to show affection towards each other, had to wait until we got in our room. That was bad for a young couple. Well, we lived through that, too. There was more to come.

We still had our friends, Bob and Ruth Bishop. By this time they had a child, a little girl named Gail. They lived in West End in a pretty subdivision named Capitol View. They lived with her parents, so I wasn't the only one with no privacy. Their reason was different. Ruth moved in with her parents when Bob was drafted and they saved in order to pay for a home, which they did.

We liked Capitol View and, when a house two doors down from our friends came up for sale, we bought it. It was a small house, but very pretty, fairly large master bedroom with private bath, two other bedrooms. That turned out to be a good move. I had my friend, Ruth, who meant so much to me and our children made lifelong friends quickly. I suppose that was the best move we ever made. We lived there seven years. During that time Wesley's diligence and hard work paid off. He began his climb to becoming a very important man. Life was easier. Rationing was still in effect, but that was no bother.

Ruth's mother was a dear and so was her father, Mattie and Will. Mattie had an old gear shift car, I mean the kind that you had to push the clutch in, change the gears by hand, the ones in the floor board on the stick. Well, Mattie could drive it if someone was dying or something like that, but as a regular thing, no. So, twice a week when rationed meat or Coca-Colas were delivered to the grocery store, I drove. We really had fun those days. I do believe those were the first days of my liberation. Being around people, I became a person—and found out that I was pretty again. We had interesting neighbors; Ellen and Fred Miller, and the Stuckeys and their four children. Sarah Stuckey became Elaine's lifelong friend as did Mary Ellen Miller and Ann Love who lived two doors down.

Somewhere I developed some fears while living on Clay Street. I know now where they started and why. In that house I felt abandoned by my husband and it took me a long, long time to recover. I was afraid of storms, even intruders, which I cannot explain. Mabel and

I found out after she moved into the Capitol View house that living together was not possible. So, she moved out, which was the best thing for her. Maybe she had some hang-ups after her mother died.

Perhaps Capitol View was so happy because Peggy was born while we lived there. At first I did not know how I was ever going to be able to handle another baby. For one thing I did not have an obstetrician with my other babies, so I had natural childbirth. I was mortally afraid. I did not see how I could go through all of that pain. Besides, Sam, my youngest was eleven years old and he'd been an extremely difficult baby to have. His head was, according to the doctor's words, the size of a grapefruit when it should have been the size of an orange. No fun!

Elaine and Anita were nearly fourteen and seventeen and were dating. I knew they would be embarrassed that their 'old' mother was pregnant. I was thirty-five and had lived so long I thought I was old, too! Well, along came Peggy, the most perfect baby in the world. We all loved her. She is, along with my other children and marrying Wesley, the best thing that ever happened in my life.

We lived in Capitol View for seven years. Our next move was Wesley's idea. Cotton Producers was building a new office building on Peachtree Road across from Lenox Square, which was new, and he wanted to be nearer plus he was fast moving up and would soon become general manager of Gold Kist. Cotton Producers changed its name when he became executive vice president and general manager.

Back when we'd moved from the Arnolds' home, we'd made quite a big step by moving to Woodland Avenue in East Atlanta. Of course, we were renting. But we had found a lovely, three-room, brick duplex. The rooms were spacious and we had great neighbors. Elaine was just starting to walk. And, looking back, I'd say those were happy days. Wesley's mother was still living. So, Mabel and Elsie had a place to live. Wesley was getting raises in salary along and we knew we were on our way. We lived there until the people on the other side bought it and wanted to live in our side because it was the nicest. The husband had a good job, but got noisy drunk almost every night he was at home. He also mistreated his wife. She was a nice lady and always forgave him afterwards. We all know those stories. Wesley got enough of his yelling and slamming things around. So, he asked him to move. We may have been renting the entire house and they were paying us rent. I believe that was the way it was. Well, we received a letter in a day or so asking us to move. This man had bought the house. We would have been happy there for a while, so we were disappointed. However, it was funny.

Next, we'd moved into the apartment house near Ponce de Leon, and then the duplex on Oakland Avenue. That was the place where Elaine's little Easter duck got eaten by a rat, which explains the rapid move to the five-room house on McPherson Avenue where Anita was born. We were coming up in the world enough to hire a woman to help take care of me and the baby, and Elaine, who was not quite three. The lady we got was so nice and kind, but the scariest looking person you have ever seen. We had not seen her before we hired her from the agency. Anyway, she was great with the babies but we came to find out that she had just gotten out of jail. Her face had been cut up at some time in her life. However, we got along fine, she loved us all. The only thing was she told Wesley in no uncertain terms that she couldn't cook with the meager supply of pans that I had. So, he bought her an entire set of stainless steel. She paid him back by cooking great meals.

Sam was born while we lived on Clay Street. He had a pretty rough time getting here and actually only had a few good years in his entire life. He was a beautiful, curly headed child, a happy disposition, sensitive and smart. However, he developed diabetes when he was eleven years old and had it rough from then on. Sam was an active, regular boy, wanted to do all of the things that boys did, had a great zest for life. But as he got older, he knew that just wasn't the way it was going to be. He managed through high school with just the usual complicated twists of diabetes. Well, no, he had some bad times. His case was more brittle than most and if his sugar was not balanced and other things he was in deep trouble. Once during the night, I heard glass breaking. So, I ran into his bathroom and found him on the floor convulsing. Fortunately, Wesley was at home to help. We gave him glucose and tried not to kill him at the same time because he couldn't swallow. God, that was terrifying. From that time on I lived on ready, never really knowing peace as far as his health was concerned.

I believe our children were happiest when we lived in Capitol View. They all had many friends and Elaine has kept in touch with five of her very best friends all these many years. She was in the fourth grade when we moved there and we were still there when she entered the University of Georgia. I remember feeling so old because she was my first child to leave. Mary Ellen Miller, her close friend went also and, one morning, her mother Ellen called to say she would bring the handkerchiefs if I would just cry with her. So that's what we did. That was just the beginning because, of course, they all left.

We had really talked up college to Peggy, who was around two years old because we knew she would miss Elaine and wonder where she was. She was excited about going with us to take Elaine, not knowing what to expect, just knowing that she was going to this very important place. Sometime before we were to leave for Athens, Peggy developed a high fever, 105, during the night. So, we took her to the hospital thinking it might be meningitis. Thank God, it wasn't. Bless her baby heart, when she finally got a little better, she asked me, "Are we at college?" We lived through all of that.

When Anita was a senior in high school we found a house across town in Buckhead. We had been looking for about one year, thinking that when Anita did graduate would be the time to move closer to Wesley's office now in Buckhead. We talked it over, knowing it would be hard on Anita. But she thought she could drive that distance every day. (That was a big mistake on our part.) Anyway, we moved and Anita had a terrible time making everything work. It would have been much easier for Wesley to have driven back and forth than for an inexperienced sixteen-year-old. I regret making that move.

Elaine was doing quite well at the University of Georgia until she met a handsome boy named Buddy Herron. She was always the romantic and when she and Buddy got better acquainted and discovered that they had played in the same playpen when they were babies, that did it! Buddy's parents had been our friends for years but we had lost touch for a few years. His mother and her family had grown up living next door to Wesley and his family. They were all good friends. Wesley helped Ray (Buddy's mother) with her paper route. Then when we were married, since we all attended the same church, we drifted into a good friendship. We had dinner together and that sort of thing. Elaine and Buddy got into this hot relationship, thinking God or fate or something had planned it that way and so why finish school when they were so much in love. Wesley was dead set against it, and he was so right. They were sophomores at the time. I didn't encourage it, but I must admit, I thought my children could do no wrong and should be happy at all times. So, I really didn't fight it. Buddy was as much of a child as Elaine, had no way of making a living except to go to work for his father who was in the printing business in Decatur. His mother also worked there, so he was really back in the fold again, not his own person by any means. The business was not prosperous and had no future. So, Elaine and Buddy got off to a bad start. Elaine was such a believing young person. When she made a friend, they could do no wrong and you dare not say they could.

Buddy's father in his youth had been a handsome man with a good singing voice. He sang in church quartets, etc. Finally, when his children were almost grown, he became a Baptist preacher in a small church. He and Ray, the mother, were good people, but that wasn't enough to help keep the young marriage going. Elaine and Buddy decided to marry and leave school, which they did. Since we had recently moved and all of her friends were in Capitol View, Elaine wanted to marry in the Capitol View church across town. What a job that was! I tell you, that last move was fast becoming a headache.

Sammy adjusted very well. He enrolled in Northside High School and made friends easily. He loved sports and had tried to play football when he was in Sylvan High. However, he broke one of his legs, so that ended his football career. I dreaded the day that he would go to the university in Athens because I knew the wild things that went on there. A good, healthy boy could weather all of that and, as a rule, live through it. I knew that Sam could not eat some things and certainly not drink much. I also knew that he would. He managed a year and a half and then the trouble began. It may have happened anyway, but Sam wanted some of everything and was determined to have it. This isn't too bad, but we received a letter from the dean saying that he had been seen during a "panty raid". If you think about it, I suppose a lot of letters went out because Sam couldn't have been the only one on the raid. But we were not happy about our letter. Anyway, he was sampling a lot of things in Athens. The heartbreak of all heartbreaks was about to happen.

I suppose I had better set the scene for this part of our life. We had made the move from Capitol View to Pine Lake Drive, north of Buckhead, a big move up for us. Wesley was going places in Gold Kist, still working hard but was making a name for himself in agriculture throughout the nation. He was still a very young man, only 41 years old, a good father and husband, very generous with his family. I remember buying a red knit dress, perhaps paying forty dollars for it, not a lot, but enough for those days. I was a little hesitant about getting it and mentioned it to Wesley. His words were, "Don't worry, I will buy you all the red dresses you want." And he meant it.

We, as a couple, were very happy. We had grown up, had lived through some hard times, both emotionally and monetarily, guess you might say we had weathered a lot of storms.

Elaine's wedding was lovely and, even though they were very young, we hoped they would be happy.

Anita and Sammy were in school in Athens. She was doing very well, had made lots of friends, was in sorority activities, had pretty clothes and always looked and acted pretty. I really believe Anita enjoyed being in college. Her grades were good and she just seemed to be happy. Sam drove her crazy because they shared a car. Anita's friends all liked Sammy because he was a fun pest, though he also borrowed money from Anita and maybe her friends.

Peggy was only two when we moved to Pine Lake Drive and three when Elaine married. She was pretty much grown from the very beginning. She must have had a hard time figuring out just where she fit with all of those grownup people. She attended Fritz

Orr nursery school and kindergarten, never wanted to get on that school bus, though. (Later Peggy told me that it was because Tracy Clute threw up almost every morning on the bus.) I hated to make her, but the lady bus driver seemed to know what she was doing when she finally told me, "Be firm, Mrs. Paris." I didn't mention that I had the same problem with Anita when she started to school. I suppose I was doing something wrong. But if I was, I kept on doing it, a slow learner, I guess. They all managed to grow up self-assured, so maybe my way wasn't all bad.

Peggy had a little friend who lived across the street, Bertie McDonald, and also another friend down a few doors, so she was not lonely. She entered The Lovett School when she became old enough and had wonderful school years all the way through high school, made lots of friends and took advantage of being able to go to such an outstanding school. She finished the University of Georgia in three and a half years. The main reason was that she fell in love with Jim and wanted to get married, which she did. They had a wonderful marriage, but more about that later. While we're thinking about Peggy, though, let me say that she has been a joy and a blessing to the entire family.

Our life on Pine Lake was good. We loved the house, it was roomy and pretty with a big corner lot that Wesley enjoyed working in. He turned a new yard into a thing of beauty with a new lighted patio and loads of flowers. I must mention that our lovely flagstone patio was built over our septic tank, we later found this out. This was the first time that Wesley had gardened except for a Victory Garden of cabbage when we lived on Clay Street. You can only eat so much cabbage, so his garden finally rotted and started smelling up the neighborhood. Oh, well, he tried.

We lived a short distance from Chastain Park where wonderful musicals and plays were performed. We loved that. We were also not far from The Red Barn Inn, the best steak in the world. Even though Peggy was a wee one, we all went often and enjoyed those times.

Shopping was the best, not far from Buckhead, the best area in Atlanta, a short drive to the best grocery store. Oh, yes, by that time

I had a car that we didn't have to sell, had had it for a year or so on Shannon Drive in Capitol View. It was beautiful, a hard top Buick, just lovely. Actually life was good. Wesley and I managed to take one trip, a business trip to the Greenbrier, I believe, leaving Anita, who was in college, in charge. She had a friend also her age, Sandra, who stayed to help her. That didn't work out too well. Sam didn't cooperate and Peggy gave them a hard time. Perhaps that was not a good idea. Also they became afraid during the night and locked everyone in one room. I guess they weren't as old as I thought. Never mind, we had many more wonderful trips later.

Wesley kept me informed about what was going on in Gold Kist. He had the second most important job and Mr. Brooks had him in line to succeed him. However, it was not all fun and games. Gold Kist was fast becoming one of the best run and largest farmers' coops in the south or maybe the country. So, you can imagine the stress he was under. It was fun, but he had to stay on this toes.

Our only problem was Sammy's health. As he got older, he became more independent. I couldn't control his every move and his temperament was not conducive to control anyway. That was Sam's charm, but, Lord, it was hard to deal with. From about that time on our entire lives depended on Sam's health. The whole family was affected by it, and it got much worse.

# CHAPTER
# SEVEN

## How Would You Like to Go to Russia?

Let's talk about my travels and how they got started. I believe we've settled the very fact that I married a brilliant man. I believed most everything he said. So, one afternoon I was standing in the foyer of our beautiful house on Foxcroft Road and he came home from work to say something I found hard to believe, "How would you like to go on a trip to Russia?" I believed him as usual, just didn't know how this could be. So my answer was, "When?"

Wesley and Bill Gaston from his office had often travelled abroad to visit different poultry places—the near east, the far east, all over the world—and Wesley had brought back all sorts of gifts for me; a lovely scarf, silver ash trays, a diamond ring from Holland, a lovely solitaire. But this trip was something else. Russia! And via Paris!

Peggy was twelve years old and wanted to go to an exclusive camp, we thought. Later on we found out that she had wanted to go with us. We really didn't know this. The camp was expensive, perhaps as much as the trip would have been.

Not knowing her wants, each day around five o'clock I would write to her telling her most of what had happened to us that day, thinking that she would save those notes and we would put them together for a travel book. Not so, she was upset because she hated the camp. If you are not a "camp kid," you are just not a "camp kid." This made me feel so bad because I really did miss her.

But the trip was so good. One really should go to Paris with someone you love. I remember Wesley wanted to take me to a speakeasy and he kept telling me if it got too rough just say so and we would leave. Well, it did get a little rough, but I stuck it out until the bitter end. On the way back to our hotel the taxi driver told Wesley that he would never take his wife to one of those shows. I really did not mind too much.

While we were still in France, the trip to Russia was cancelled, so we decided to go to Italy, get a visa and go on to the Holy Land. That took time. So, we saw Italy. Then on to the Holy Land.

Italy was just like you've read about, beautiful models walking, hugging and kissing. They had to be movie stars or someone glamourous, so beautiful, well dressed, high heeled beauties. Then the shops and their windows! I bought a black suede coat and a hat trimmed in white mink. Somewhere along the way we ended up in Pompeii among the ancient ruins. And I bought a very pretty cameo. These things I still have and they are in good shape. We loved Italy just like we'd loved France.

We boarded a plane to the Holy Land. Some nice black ladies sat in back of us and you never heard such exclamations. Every time we swooped down over something of interest from the Bible and finally landed in Jerusalem, bedlam really broke loose, yelling and screaming, nothing at all holy, not just from the black ladies but from everyone on the ground meeting the plane.

We had a guide to tour Jerusalem. It was interesting but hot and dirty, always noisy. I didn't understand the time of prayers as I do now after a little more study.  One day as we were touring we saw a rug shop run by a little man, kind of fat, in diamonds and a silk suit. I saw an antique nine-by-twelve rug of many colors. Beautiful! He wanted five hundred dollars for it. A bargain! Wesley was willing to buy it but he did question how I knew how to buy it—what did I know about oriental rugs? Especially an antique one made by just one family? Well, I just did. We went home and waited six months and it finally came in good condition. I used it in our home for around forty years. Then as I moved around after Wesley died I did not have a place to put it, so I gave it to Elaine for her bedroom or wherever she wanted to use it. It made her already beautiful apartment even more beautiful. A dealer in antique rugs from Macy's wanted to buy all of my rugs but except this one: it was too valuable. So, it was a good buy.

Two or three years later, we did go to Russia and this time we took Peggy with us. That was a trip to remember. As we boarded the plane, we were given an apple and, believe it or not, that was our food for the whole long, long Aeroflot flight. We boarded one at a time, they did not trust anyone. And we had some fun, interesting people on that flight. One couple was so good looking. She had a hat box full of wigs of different sorts. I mean, she dressed up even though we were told not to overdress since the Russians were very poor at that time. Let's face it, this young woman was the star and her husband loved it.

As we landed and checked into our hotel we were given a tour guide for the entire trip who was young and had a fun mind of her own. She kept saying, "Uh-oh, there's Big Brother." We had quite a tour of Moscow, including one day a trip to the ballet that Wesley didn't care for and tried to leave. Nyet, comrade! They made him go back in. Wesley was not used to being made to do anything, but back in it was.

That was an interesting trip. The food was pretty, no ice for drinks or water and the towels for bathing were like dirty dish towels, probably not dirty, just faded and thin. It was the best that they had at that time. After that I understand that things got much better. The people were friendly. Men wanted to dance with Peggy and me, but each time Wesley said no.

Let me add, before we left home Peggy and I took a short course in the Russian language. Peggy did much better than I did. I could read okay. But since she had studied language in school, not Russian but French, she was better at it than I was.

Sunday came and in order to go to church we went by taxi to a big building that had different services for churches of all faiths.

They gave us a pretty young girl to sit behind us and interpret the service. I called her my angel on my shoulder. When we started back to the hotel some ladies wanted us to go with them to the back grounds of the building. I think they wanted their picture taken with us because we were an oddity. And when we did, that didn't happen because someone said to leave because the police were coming. And, sure enough, as we were leaving, the police did come. We were not bothered because we had already left the building.

On the trip home we boarded a bus, and even though we were not searched, the bus was not allowed to leave for the airport until somebody came up with, I believe, a little jar or something that was missing from one of the rooms, a souvenir, I guess. Well, a woman finally came up with it and we took off. We boarded one by one with our passport in hand. Smart Alec me came up to the fellow letting me saying, "Yep, that's me." When that plane took off, it didn't leave an inch of the run way behind. We all stood up and yelled, "Hooray." I'm sure they were good pilots, but at the time it was a guess. That was one flight we were glad when it was over.

When we got home, we found that Sam had been busy and had thrown a great big party. Our house was intact, I believe, because of Nellie. The only thing missing was my electric curlers from one of the bathrooms. Electric curlers were new at that time. Actually we were happy that was all.

My husband really knew his way around this world. I almost left out Peru. He had made one trip to Lima before he took me because they, Gold Kist, owned an anchovy fleet of boats and for some reason could only keep them afloat a certain number of hours a day. He thought it wise to take his lawyers and bankers on this fantastic trip to Peru. And I got to go. How lucky, or I might say fortunate, can you get?

One part of the trip that I could have taken but didn't because he had already done it was to go up the famous mountain, Machu Picchu. I should have gone anyway even though he did not want to go again, but I did not want to go alone. He had suffered from shortness of breath, a hard part of the trip.

Those folks in Lima really could have a party and they had one for us—wonderful food and music, the waiters dressed in great looking uniforms and white gloves. When some of them had visited us before our trip there, we thought we had a nice party for them. And it was just that, a nice party, but nothing like what they had for us. When we left Lima at the airport, I said in my usual friendly way, "Well, y'all come." And, believe me, they did, a few at a time, just beautiful people.

On Wesley's first trip there he bought me three yards of vicuna at one hundred dollars a yard to have a coat made. It was so valuable they kept it in a bank vault. I later did have a tailor in Buckhead make one for me. After I moved to St. George, I gave it to Sally, my granddaughter. I know she is enjoying it. That fabric was made famous when some people in Washington made a big to-do about some stain or other on a coat.

On our trip around the world we took Mark, Elaine's son, as well as Peggy. He was just twelve years old and Peggy fifteen or sixteen. It was great fun having them along and seeing things through their eyes. I remember one cute thing Mark did when Wesley told him he could call room service and order anything he wanted. He called the lobby and said, "Ring me up to room service, please."

Also each of us took turns on Sunday nights selecting places to eat. One Sunday night Peggy decided on a place and it turned out to be the most expensive place around. He, her daddy, just laughed and she ordered lobster. Fun!

We watched the Changing of the Guard. These things were new to us and more formal. After England, of course, came France. Paris, the Louvre, a once in a lifetime opportunity to see such artwork.

Later, when Mark was eighteen and in the Navy, he was on a ship that went around the world. He wrote me a postcard to tell me about it saying, yes, he had been around the world again but nowhere near as deluxe as our trip. This time he took his friends into the lobbies of these beautiful hotels that he had enjoyed before. That was as far as they could go. We were so happy that we had let him see the best of everything. He dove off the high board of a pool in India. This boy saw the world in a hurry with us. He was just about to ride a young elephant when that same elephant raised his trunk and slapped a boy across the field. No ride for Mark. He was disappointed, but also glad he missed that part. This happened in Bangkok.

This trip was not all fun and games. We were away from home for six weeks and Mark got a little homesick and when his father, Buddy, wrote him a letter, it didn't help. Buddy had never been away from home, at least not that often, and certainly not on a trip like this one. And I suppose he was afraid something might happen to Mark. I believe since I really loved Mark and had cared for him a lot since he was small that I was able to help him get over his homesickness. Anyway, we made it back home just fine.

I did worry about Mark and Peggy. I realized that Peggy had to share her parents and, even though we loved having Mark, I'm sure Peggy could have enjoyed being the only kid on parts of that trip. But it all worked out and they are now both grown and love each other.

# A LIFE
## IN
# PICTURES

✵

Margaret Oldham,
Helen's mother.

Wesley Paris,
Helen's husband

# Helen and Wesley

Helen, Wesley, and Elaine

Helen with Elaine and Anita

With Elaine, Sam,
and Anita at Clay Street

Anita, Sam, and Elaine

# Hal at the beach

# Hal in World War Two

Helen (in the middle) with her sisters
June and Margaret

# Helen at home

# Helen with Peggy

# Helen in the 1950s

Helen in 1967

Helen with Dana, Mark, and Lee

Helen with her grandchildren

# Helen with her daughters

# PART
# TWO

1968-2017
## SNAPSHOTS FROM
## A LIFE

A most pleasant surprise just happened to me. Rodney McLean, my nephew, called from Montana. He and I only seem to see each other at funerals. He is absolutely the best-looking man, happy, laughs at your "funnies," that type, friendly, outgoing. We always called him Dub, I suppose because he looked so very much like his father who died at a young age. That was his nickname and it stuck until he grew up and married. Since he is known by his adult name of Rodney, I am going to call him that.

Rodney married a wonderful, darling girl and they had five children. I have met them but, since they live so far away and I'm bad about keeping up with folks, I really do not know them as I would like. Rodney is my middle sister's oldest child. We're going to keep in touch. I am the last one to remain alive in my family of six. That's one reason I am writing this book, to try to help the ones coming after me to know something of their roots. None of my family kept a record of any sort. If I don't write it, it dies.

Rodney and Jimmie Ann live in Kalispell, Montana. My sister June, Rodney's mother, lived in Lake Charles, Louisiana with her husband Flip. June and Flip had four children, two boys and two girls. No wonder they are all so good looking—their parents were the best-looking, most fun, and cutest folks around. Flip was in World War II and I believe he was a paratrooper like my brother, Hal. When Flip died very young, we had hoped that June would move back to

Atlanta. However, she didn't. Her home and her friends were in Lake Charles and, once you get Louisiana in your blood, that's it.

⊗

Making my mind up about moving in to St. George made me have trouble sleeping, which is pretty unusual for me. The trouble is that, while the figures told me that I could afford to come here, I still felt unsure.

I'd had emergency surgery about three months before that was quite serious, an intestinal blockage that came on at two-thirty on a Wednesday night—lots of pain and, when it was all over, very scary. I am well now but realize that if it happens again—and it can, even though Dr. Rosen says it's not likely—I need to be in a place such as St. George. As it was, I was in Northside Hospital for eight days, then went to Anita and Guy's for another eight days and then home feeling tough for another four or five weeks. My girls were so good to me. Anita and Guy couldn't have been better, Peggy brought in food, Elaine was thoughtful. They all came to my aid. However, I know it will be better, no matter what happens, not to have to call on family but to be more independent.

What made it so bad was my timing was off. Jim, Peggy's husband, had just died about two months earlier. It seems that blood did not get to his heart and he died instantly as he was getting out of the shower, so sad and unexpected. Peggy was simply devastated, we all were, but deeply saddened for her. After Jim's death—about three weeks, I believe (time got so mixed up)—Lee, Elaine's middle son, died in his sleep from an insulin reaction. He had been in St. Simons Island earlier and had fallen while having another insulin reaction, breaking his collarbone. The doctors did not think it wise to operate because his health was so poor. What a shock to lose your grandchild! Lee and Mark had spent some time living with us during Elaine and Buddy's divorce years ago and I felt that they were part mine. Then Mabel died a few days later. Her death was not unexpected since she had Altzheimer's. Then Guy's father shortly after. He did not seem to be in such bad health, but since several things were wrong, I suppose it was just too much. He was 94 years old but certainly did not look it. Mabel was 90, and since her disease was so bad, she was miserable, so it seemed better.

St. George is really a lovely place to live, a little costly, but worth it. Since I am writing this for future members of our family and economics all over the world will very likely change by the time this is read, I may as well tell what it costs. I have a three-room apartment which is very pretty, with a large living/library type room, lots of books, plenty of light, ten-foot ceilings, and one bedroom. I must say it could be a little larger since I have large furniture that I simply could not part with. A tiny bathroom with all the fixings, so it's fine. A small kitchen in which I had hardwood flooring installed, black appliances, a chandelier, really quite pretty and very elegant. Also a porch—which in my mind is a lifesaver since I love the outdoors and the spacious feeling it gives.

Since this is a retirement village, the building and grounds take up an entire block. So, besides being lovely to look at, it is comfortable and spacious. It offers everything needed to make life enjoyable. Fairly good food, some days better than others, but all in all pretty good. I must stress, since it is very important to me, that it is well managed and kept clean.

We have entertainment of all kinds. Something goes on every day, exercise classes, great places to walk when the weather allows. Everything is furnished for this amount except the telephone. My expenses here are three thousand dollars a month. The additional fee to buy (not fee simple) any apartment was two hundred thousand four hundred dollars. This may be of no interest to all of you, the readers, just letting you know what things are costing these days for folks that are retired and not ready for a nursing home.

When I first moved to St. George, of course people got sick and some of them died, but since I had not lived here long enough to make lasting friends, these deaths were just people. But now they are my friends! That's what makes the difference. My good friend, Margaret McWhorter, died after a long illness. We had been neighbors in Dunwoody for 23 years. Her husband is 90 years old and still living. I need to pay him more attention, like having dinner more often. He eats with the same man who is not the best company around and that's not good for Tom since he was used to more interesting people.

Another friend appears to be dying, or at least that is what she says every time I go to see her, which was every day for a while.

Two more deaths to tell about and then I'm done with the sad news. Pat Dawson died last year after a long, depressing illness. For about four years she did not know anyone and was in skilled nursing. I knew her very well since my daughter, Peggy, and her son, Jim, had been married for over thirty years before his death. One more, and that's it, Don Sands, CEO of Gold Kist for about ten years, he was one of four men to succeed my husband.

Dana and Pete (Anita's oldest and her husband) came for lunch. We ended up looking at old pictures, snapshots of Dana's mother, Anita. Old picture albums can bring lots of memories back into a life that I am the only one old enough to remember. These albums tell stories of their own.

My husband was so very young. I was also, but somehow I didn't think so. I remember telling him, "I'll be so glad when you're thirty years old." His answer was, "Don't say that, then you will be an old lady." He meant nothing by saying that and didn't even realize the truth of his statement. Even though I was one year younger than he was, the general consensus was and still is men are more attractive as they grow older than women.

I enjoyed being with Dana and Peter. They are bright, interesting and very talented young people. They live in Los Angeles and are in the creative acting, writing and movie business. Peter is well into his career and Dana is fast making her way. She is so modest it's hard to tell where she is.

We are so fortunate in that we have a lot of creative talent in our family, Matt, so bright, loves music, Laura is a gifted artist, Peggy can do all sorts of things, makes money by being a court reporter but could easily have another career or two in decorating or party giving. Anita, very talented, wears about eight hats in her work, makes speeches and excels with people. Our family is large and each one has their own abilities. Elaine is forever young at sixty-six. She has been divorced for years and is still matching wits with her former husband, Joe. She has had a tough time dealing with him financially but has won out so far. She keeps perfect records and will win eventually.

I went to my dream class this morning and told my dream. The way the class works is one person tells or reads their dream and the others try to figure out what the dream means. The dream that I told was entitled, "Not Needed Child." I had left my baby with my mother for several months because I would either forget or just did not pick her up. I kept putting off getting her, all the time feeling guilty. I would start to get her and then something would happen and I just didn't. I worried for fear she would not remember who I was. When I told my dream to the class, I didn't mention that I finally did go by my mother's house to get her and I remember now how very strange the feeling was. The baby really did not know me.

The class had all sorts of explanations for my dream but none of them were even close. I felt like a game show host on TV. Finally, Talullah, our teacher, made a little summation that included me being the mother, both mothers, and also the baby. She explained that is how dreams are all encompassing. So, she was getting there. Finally I explained that I was the baby and it really did happen to me. I was older, fourteen, but nothing was explained to me at the time. I was left for my grandmother to finish raising me. Actually I felt abandoned all of my life, especially after my mother married my stepfather. I didn't tell my class that I had come to terms with it – really could not have talked about it otherwise. This class has helped me in several ways, that and getting old. I see the meaning of so many different happenings in my life. It bothers me that I have waited years by not doing some of the things I now do to gain that peace. It doesn't come quickly or even easily.

It's taken me a long time to realize that the strong bond between mother and child will be around as long as you live even though sometimes you do not even want it. It's something you cannot escape.

My brothers and sisters had it easier than I because they accepted it and I fought it. Don't tell me it's time for me to die simply because I can understand things about life better. It's high time I did, for goodness sake.

⧼⧽

Helen was dying. She was on no life support, just oxygen. Helen was my brother John's wife of many years. They married twice, the last time about one year earlier. They had been divorced for fifteen years, though she said her church did not believe in divorce, and so claimed they were still married. She still kept up with the comings and goings of her family, went to Lake Charles, LA, to my sister June's funeral, visited in her home a few months earlier and just wouldn't give up. Well, she won because they remarried in her church with all of the fixings.

My friend, Ben, drove us to the wedding. And would you believe, we got lost and missed the service? We made it for the reception. But I was so frustrated, actually mad at Ben even though it wasn't his fault. I'd been looking forward to their wedding because I knew Johnny was lonely. During the separation period he was involved with a younger woman. They were very close even though they lived in separate houses. He was so devoted and, since her mother finally died, probably would have gotten married except she became ill with cancer and died. How very sad for him.

This woman, Ann, left John pretty well off financially, a lovely house without a mortgage and a monthly income. I know her sister was fit to be tied that he remarried Helen.

Helen and John had been married for six months when Helen was diagnosed with ovarian cancer. They have had a tough time of it, chemotherapy did no good. So, they went to Mexico for some cure that they had heard about, just grasping at straws, I guess. Their preacher went along and stayed with them for the entire three-week period. That trip proved to be a disaster because she ended up in Northside Hospital soon after to have built up fluid removed. The day she was preparing to leave for home she suffered a stroke.

While I was at Northside Hospital visiting, John started talking.

It's funny how someone can be lying in bed dying and people can carry on a conversation as though nothing unusual is going on. Helen's niece was also there, a pretty girl, maybe twenty years old. She was so interested in what John and I were talking about, "the good old days." He started off telling me about the time in Melbourne when they had no place to live, they being our mother and four children, Hal, June, John and Margaret. Somehow, they moved into a house vacated by its owners for the summer on what is called The Bluff, a lovely area by the Indian River where the wealthy folks lived. As I have said before, my mother was a very enterprising woman. So, they found themselves living in this lovely house, furniture and all. Apparently, they mixed their few pieces in with the fine stuff. (I knew they lived on The Bluff but it never dawned on me that they were squatters.) I'm sure they had no electricity, nothing to cook on. So, they tore boards off of either that house or another one for wood to cook with in the back yard. I'm sure the people were surprised when they returned home for the winter to see their house trashed.

The same group lived in Macon for a year or so. John was just a little boy but found a farmer to work for. Well, this farmer told John that if he worked during the farm season he would pay him in full at the end of the season, harvest time. In the meantime, after John had completed his share of the bargain, John and family moved back to Atlanta. At harvest time John received a letter from the farmer saying that the harvest had been poor and this was Depression time, which no doubt was true, that he could not pay in money. However, since John had kept his end of the bargain and had worked hard he was going to give him old Annie, the horse that John had used to plow with, and Haney, the cat that John was so crazy about, but—and he was so sorry—old Annie got sick and died and Haney was not eating and was looking poorly, so he had better hurry on down and get her. Poor John!

When Helen died, I thought how strange it is how death makes the victim immediately old. When I saw Helen a year earlier at the wedding reception, she looked young and pretty even though she was sixty-six or seven. Well, the undertaker will probably make her look young again. But that doesn't count, does it?

John apparently did get mixed up with Ann long before he and Helen divorced. All of this was news to me. Ann was only eighteen when she went to work for the same company that employed Helen. John was hired to set up the computers for the same company and became interested in Ann, who visited in John and Helen's home and, as things go, got involved with John and stayed that way for around fifteen years before the divorce. My, my!

John had lost two loves to cancer. Ann died several years ago of stomach cancer, now Helen of ovarian cancer. How can all of this happen to a shy little nine-year-old boy who came to my house crying because some boys were bothering him? I was pregnant but went out and chased them anyway.

John only went to the seventh grade of school, so actually he has done pretty well. School was not the most important item of our lives.

Peggy and Laura went with me to Helen's funeral. And, as things always happen when I go in the direction of Austell, I get lost but good! We allowed what we considered plenty of time but ended up making it a hard, long journey. We barely made it in time to go to the room where John was and speak to him. Nothing like being relaxed.

Prophecy Church is a nice, plain little country church on a pretty lot. One of these days they will have a new church because, like most churches, they are working on a building fund.

We were not late. However, the church was full. So, the usher led us up front to the choir loft, my first time sitting behind the preacher. I suppose the church held one hundred and fifty people. I love little country churches. This one was so natural, what you saw was what you got. As folks came in the usher quite audibly said, "Come on down" and would find some kind of seat for them. The service started a little late. As usual, in these little churches the flowers were beautiful, and lots of them, too. There is something about all of those flowers at a funeral that doesn't really express my feelings, but I do understand them. People really want to show their sympathy. Somehow, to me, flowers in such large quantities just make the occasion that much sadder, especially the next day on the grave, they are dead. The duet sang in a sweet country twang about, "I want to be with Jesus". They sang two songs. Both were sweet and sad and hopeful. Two preachers talked glowingly of Helen, then the burial in the cemetery behind the church. Quite a nice little uneventful service for a nice little uneventful lady!

❦

As they get older and perhaps nearer to meeting their maker, some folks say, "Oh, I never worry." They claim they'll be ready whenever God calls.

Well, I'm ready too, to a certain extent. But I suppose I can't get that said without a little worry. My worry is mixed up with a lot of prayers knowing full well that when God is ready for me—or, I should say, I am ready for him—He will take me. Anyway, I feel grateful to have a little longer to enjoy the "now." My last complete heart examination happily came out perfect. This examination consisted of four tests starting out with a telephone pacemaker test that I have each month to make sure my pacemaker is functioning as it should. Everything turned out just fine. I suppose I should be ashamed to have worried.

I am still happy at St. George Village. All is well here as far as I am concerned. The food still can't make up its mind whether to be good or bad—it's sort of even right now. I've gotten somewhat used to the goings on here. The activities get better all the time, classes in health, classes in growing old, even a class on computers—they claim it's an easy one. That remains to be seen since I have struggled along with one for nearly a year and never did conquer it. Maybe if I wait long enough, computers will be simple enough even for me. I say this with tongue in cheek because I am pretty sure with a little help I can manage. I didn't have any help with Apple when they first came out. But people should understand how difficult it can be for an old dog to learn new tricks.

St. George also offers all sorts of exercise classes. I'm taking Tai Chi, yoga, stretch and aerobics and starting line dancing next week. My doctors are sure that is what keeps me so healthy. My cardiologist is sold on exercise for the functioning heart to keep it strong—that and paying attention to diet. These are things that I believe in—plenty of exercise, at least one hour daily, plus walking one mile every day. I also work on floor exercise, not every day but as time and energy allow, to keep my knees in good shape by doing different leg lifts almost every day. And you have to pay attention to the diet: Low sugar and salt, at least eight fruits and vegetables, small servings of fish or lean meat, skim milk on high fiber cereal, whole wheat bread instead of white. As a matter of fact, stay away altogether from white foods like bread, potatoes, rice, and pasta. Sounds like I stay busy just staying alive, doesn't it? It has become a way of life with me, so I do not have to spend a lot of time thinking about it. Oh, and the water—at least six glasses a day. Most evenings, I drink one-half a glass of white wine. I need to switch to red, I'm told, so perhaps I will.

I have good sleeping habits that work well most of the time. In order to do this, I go to bed early, around eight o'clock, always read a little gold devotional book that a friend gave me nine years ago when I developed breast cancer. I just read one page a night since I almost know it by memory. I have made a pretty strict habit of turning off my music and going to sleep by ten o'clock. Most of the time this works, not always. I believe sleep is most important, that it keeps your brain working and your body healthy looking and feeling. All of these things manage in a big way to keep skin, hair, body weight and health in pretty good shape. Almost forgot to mention meditation, some form most every day. I try to stick to these good rules most every day, even though I believe that sometimes rules are meant to be broken and that perfection is not always beautiful. But I do firmly believe that what you do, think and say will invariably show in your face. And since we all strive to look pleasing to others and to ourselves—happiness is contagious—it behooves us to do our best and be thoughtful and kind to others. And keep in mind that your face reflects your thoughts and anger can really ruin you.

Two of my friends at St. George have recently asked me about heart health (you will notice I said heart health, not heart problems.) Angie called to say that she was told by her doctor that she needed a pacemaker. And since I have one and have gotten along fine, she wondered about getting one. She has an extremely serious bone problem that keeps her in a motorized chair and in constant pain. She manages beautifully, does pool exercises daily, and lives in her apartment alone. Thank goodness, I was able to allay some of her fears concerning the pacemaker. We have a similar reason for having one, irregular heartbeat, and she was told like I was that without one she could die at any time.

Yesterday Margaret, a very talented pianist, was playing piano after lunch. Some of us were gathered around singing. She plays anything, from sheet music or by ear. She is 96 years old, a beautiful woman, so smart and pleasant, the really whole person. I might add wealthy also. She has just donated thousands to St. George since she has no family. Her need from me was the name of my cardiologist. These folks seem to trust my opinion. They know I will tell it like it is or not at all.

I attend a large, very beautiful Methodist church. Today our minister's sermon was taken from the Book of Matthew. It had to do with mountain top experiences. These things so often happen to me, I seem to be in the right place at the right time. As he was talking I realized that I had had a mountain top experience just this past week! I bit the bullet and got a set of hearing aids. I was utterly amazed at the transformation since I had heard so many disparaging tales about them. Some folks could not wear them, so they kept them in a box. Others heard strange noises or their hearing had not improved because of them. So, I had apprehensive thoughts before I even gave them a chance. Almost from the day they were installed my life completely changed. These little $5,800 darlings are wonderful. I feel years younger, much more secure, much more sure of myself and confident. A new woman! Folks at St. George are anxious to know all about them, where I got them mainly. Looks like I am going to give the folks that sold them a lot of business since we are in a nest of folks that are constantly saying, "I am glad I don't have a hearing problem. But what did you say?"

Good things just seem to be coming my way these days. Stacy, our marketing director, wanted a writer friend of hers to interview me about my lifestyle. She did a very good interview and gave me a complete page in a special little newspaper for St. George, picture and all. I was well pleased since this little paper only comes out once a month and this time along with my article was an interview with a doctor and a dietician, just the three of us. This is one of the happenings at this time of my life that I am most proud of.

A good looking young couple in their late thirties lived in what I thought was a beautiful apartment in uptown Melbourne, sort of near the waterfront. You'd have thought they would be the last ones to have something like a murder happen to them.

How I came to know her, I don't know, not well, I'm sure. But one night she was going to be alone for a while—her husband was working—and wanted me to stay with her. I agreed and remember seeing, through a large window looking out from the bedrooms, her husband coming up the steps. I was not in bed, and was not planning to spend the night. Anyway, I walked home. The next day or so word got out that she had been murdered. What a surprise for all of Melbourne! The men gathered to help find the killer, my stepfather included. All we could think of was he left us unprotected with a murderer loose in that small town that had probably never had a killing. After a week or so it was decided that the husband had done it. That was the end of that, don't think it was ever solved. She was an awfully pretty young woman, so she could have gotten mixed up with someone else, there's no telling.

Back when my grandson Matt was in the 11th grade, he called me to ask me to talk to his class about the Great Depression. I guess they were studying what they thought was history, "the bad, old days." I had three days to think back and try to re-live those early days. I managed to get enough misery together to make it interesting and gave the talk. It was all so long ago that some of it turned out funny. I had almost forgotten all of those things that happen when you are growing up. Anyway, it all came back and the kids seemed to like it. They had never heard of hunger, oil lamps, no clothes, and all the other hardships that went along with the Depression.

A couple of days later my granddaughter Dana called, "Gran, I have the neatest idea for a film." She had already produced one short film that was nominated for an Academy Award a year earlier.

So, a few weeks later she arrived from Los Angeles with lots of film and material. It's lucky she has lots of friends, she had to borrow lights and most of the cameras from different friends. Her idea was to make a documentary film around the Depression showing the effect it had on two different types of women. So, she decided to use both of her grandmothers.

She decided to film me first—perhaps to get it over with—and I believe I did turn out to be the most difficult. Anyway, she and her friend Mark took an afternoon to set up the cameras and the lights. That meant moving all of my furniture around, showing all of the dust—almost made me want to move. After she took the lights out, a few days later I straightened the furniture and—what do you know?—the dust disappeared.

Poor thing, I thought she knew potential stars were difficult. I didn't mean to be. But can you imagine what those lights can do to a 77-year-old woman who thinks she looks pretty good? We had no makeup person so had to depend on my own makeup skills. Believe me, Dana knows less than I do about that. We finally got going. Dana is smart but had not done too much with lighting. She learned pretty soon to move some of the bad wrinkles out and get me sitting in the right position. So, we got started. She asked the questions and I attempted to answer them. We worked for three days. All in all she got about six and a half hours of me talking, some good, some bad, but interesting and fun for me. Both of us were exhausted. The next day after that session every time I passed by bed I would fall in.

Dana went up to Dahlonega after finishing me to do Ruth, her other grandmother. I really don't know how that turned out but I suppose it went well. For one thing, Ruth is much more patient than I am and, I suppose, easier to work with. Oh, well, it takes all kinds.

After Ruth, Dana wanted to get us both together for the final filming. I don't think that was the best part, but you never know. Maybe she'll manage to eliminate most of the undesirable parts.

We took a day to visit some of the houses that I had lived in in those early days. We found most of them, and there were one or two we didn't look for—like the Courtland Street one, the one that was next to the Ladies of the Evening House, remember? It was pretty dilapidated even back then.

We first went to Brookwood Drive and, after a little indecision on my part, we found it, a little, tiny brick bungalow. The house, of course, had changed in appearance. They had jalousied in the little front porch and the entire house was showing its age. What an emotional experience for me! I was fourteen when Gramma, Doc, Ken and I moved there from the lovely big house on Boulevard, NE.

We knocked on the door and were greeted by a really gorgeous younger woman. She was quite relaxed and asked us in. I really could not believe it was so small. They had removed a wall and, from what she said (we did not see the bedrooms), joined two bedrooms. So, instead of three, the little place only had two. The kitchen was almost not there, it was so small. However, I remember it as being adequate. They had done wonders to the back yard, very pretty, considering what they had to work with. As I remember, back when we lived there, the yard was not important. I suppose we had the grass cut but I just don't remember.

After making a few outside pictures—Dana looked like a little street urchin with that big battery belt buckled around her hips, but that is what it took to use that movie camera—we decided to shoot Jean Chapman's house on Lindberg Drive. The entire house was made of stone, inside and out. I remember it well because I visited them often. I remember a big party where one of the Townsend boys announced the guests as they came in. It was quite a production.

On we went to Boulevard, NE. We found the first house that I had lived in when we came to Atlanta in that one-seated car full of children. Would you believe it? Except for being run down, as was the entire neighborhood, that house was exactly the same. I would have known it anywhere. The hill seemed not as high, though. I know it was because the steps were the same. No one was there except a cat, or they would not answer the door. A card table was on the front porch with leftover beer cans from the night before. We could see inside into the big living room and on into the dining room, just the same, nothing that a few thousand dollars wouldn't fix. I loved seeing it. You could tell the neighborhood was trying to make a comeback. After all, sixty-five years can change houses and people. It was a mixed neighborhood now, black and white, young and old. It had a drug look about it. I could be wrong. But even though we didn't see any action, we could feel it.

We stopped at Wendy's for a baked potato and the restroom before going on to Boulevard, SE in the Grant Park area. No trouble finding the Arnold house. Wesley and I had rented two back rooms in their home when we were first married. I couldn't believe it, that house had not changed either. It was never the personality house and still wasn't. An empty house with a "For Sale" sign is what we saw, also run down. Since we couldn't get in, could only look in windows, Dana made pictures of the bleak outside. Along came two young men interested in buying it. We couldn't believe the asking price was $90,000. After a lovely chat with these fellows—they loved my story about having lived there so long ago—we walked up Berne Street (this little house was on Waldo) one block to the house on the corner that I had lived in with my grandmother, Doc, Aunt Kit and Ken before I was married. This house was still quite pretty, had been well cared for, or so it seemed. We couldn't get into the yard because of what looked like an iron fence. The gate was wrapped in a heavy chain and padlocked. They didn't plan to be surprised, so more pictures of the outside. There again, the Grant Park area had deteriorated badly, all sorts of folks roaming around, not any prosperous looking.

Now on to look for the house that Wesley and his mother and sisters had lived in before and even after we were married on Park Avenue (no, not the same Park Avenue). On the way we saw Park Avenue Baptist Church where we attended church and BYPU. Reverend L.E. Smith was pastor back then and his parsonage was next door to the church. It was still there. It and the old side of the church were pretty shabby. We didn't go inside but it seemed nice. You could tell the real old part from the just old part. None of it had the look of beautiful old, just poor old.

We had a little trouble finding the two houses that the Paris' lived in. I do believe the expressway got them. I found one house that looked familiar, so we shot it. Most of them looked alike anyway.

The little brick bungalow on Brookwood Drive is in a neighborhood where houses like it sell for $190,000. Keep in mind, these are old houses with absolutely no personality. The outsides are ugly, the insides are tiny, low ceilings, small, ugly fireplaces. The prices are all, it seems, because they are inside of the Perimeter Highway.

At St. George, another of my friends has moved down from the third floor. It's now filled with new folks. I went over to an ice cream social and saw some of my old friends, but things are moving along, so lots of new folks have moved in.

I'm reading a book that was written by Anita's husband, Guy Middleton. It is amazingly gory compared to my usual kind of reading—the Civil War, the War with the Indians, etc.—but is really good. It is selling like hotcakes, and his first book, too. It's called "McAdams."

Anita and Guy's life is quite busy, his book signings, the two little grandchildren, smart, good looking, active boys, growing like weeds. They, Anita and Guy, have been married fifty-four years. However, they are so young looking, you would never believe it. I can't believe how really good their lives are, good looking, plenty of money, beautiful home, the perfect married life made of love, hard work and good use of two sets of brains.

Dr. Helen's granddaughter, 14 years old, has come from Melbourne, Florida to what she thought, and rightly so, was the promised land, to live with her. Her granddaughter was named for Dr. Helen and she was happy to have her, not really knowing what was in store for her. It has been a while since she had had teenagers in her life but, true to her nature, she was more than willing to give it a try if, for no other reason, to help her daughter, Margaret, who was the girl's mother.

Everything was fine for several years. Keep in mind, her granddaughter was named for her and, even though she was willing to help with housework and other things, time has a way of changing even the best of things.

Of course, Dr. Helen, as she was called by her patients, knew human nature. She taught Sunday School (I should say Saturday School because her church had services on Saturday), even preached a little, very religious as she became older. She understood young and old people and was very patient most of the time with her granddaughter.

Dr. Helen usually stopped seeing her patients around five o'clock. So, one afternoon her granddaughter, Helen, met her at her office and went with her to get her car (an old Hertz) from the parking lot. Of course, she knew the attendants there. So, they bantered around, just playing. Hearing all of this, I asked her what he said. Her reply was, "You know how it is to flirt; don't you?" So, she was born to flirt. I'm sure she did her share as did my mother.

I remember parties on Courtland Street. She, my mother and at that time, I'm sure, J.A., who was my mother's boyfriend, had moved my brother, Billy, and me into the front hall with only a curtain for a door, so we heard everything, even though we were far too young.

Now for happier thoughts. I've told about living with my grandmother, Aunt Kit, Doc and Ken, such a different life for around two years, also my falling completely in love with Wesley Paris. Nothing got in the way of that, nothing that matters. I simply could not think straight. However, I wouldn't have changed it. Looking back on things, little things here at St. George really do not matter, just something to write about. I do think sometimes, how have I overcome part of my life? It left me stronger, made me better in some ways. Some of my friends did not love their husbands as I did, and still do. I look at his picture and pray that I will see him again. Now I am going to spend some time with happy writing. Here are parts of my happy life that did show me how to get on with the blessed life that God had in store for me from the very beginning.

Let's start at the very young age of four or five. My life was planned by God, and I had better understand that. Or why am I still here at this of age? He has been so good to me, helped me to stay healthy until the ripe old age of eighty-four, good looking, too. God not only loves us all but no doubt in my mind he does not mind if we try our best to look good. And I do that. Now, about good looks, don't get me wrong, he loves the ugly, crippled, sick, everyone the same, it's a personal thing. You, the person, have to have the understanding with Him. All of this bad stuff in my life, especially my early life, has certainly helped me cope with the rest of the happiness and somehow to understand how my life has unfolded.

⁂

David Brinkley died. I did not know him well but I did meet him, perhaps in Washington. Wesley was master of ceremonies at a meeting there and I was seated next to David Brinkley. When we were standing in line, waiting for the doors to open, Mr. Brinkley and I got well acquainted since we had quite a wait.

Of course, I knew who he was and I was impressed. But I was young, in my late forties and had so many things going and he was so easy and relaxed that it just seemed to be an enjoyable couple of hours. I even remember what I wore and, I must say, it was one of my best outfits, a short black cape, elbow length, with skirt to match, wonderful fabric and beautifully made (by me), so good I still have the cape after forty years! That was the day of hats and I had some good ones. This one was a Persian lamb crown, black, of course, with a white mink rolled brim. I still have the hat also. I bought it in Italy, I'll never forget that trip.

I was very much in love with my husband, and still am. However, had I not been, David Brinkley could have been the one! He was the most charming person you would ever want to be with. I remember he said—and I remember the exact words—"My wife would be jealous." Well, now he is gone and will be missed by all of the world.

One thing I have wanted to learn and to do reasonably well is jitterbug. Yes, I have always liked to dance and was able to follow my partner and to keep the beat, that sort of thing, a, pretty fair dancer, but I never learned to actually jitterbug. Dana and Pete were aware of that. So, they sent me a tape from Los Angeles one Christmas. I struggled for a while, learned a little and then left it alone for a while. After Christmas the next year I decided to go for it, either I would learn or I would give it up completely. So, I did, I not only know the basic step but a few other steps like turning out—well, maybe not out, just turning.

Ben came to dinner. I mentioned in a modest sort of way and demonstrated a little that I was a jitterbugger now. Then, since my tape player is upstairs, I asked him if he would like to go up and perhaps we would learn how to turn the right way. I knew Ben had been sick for about two months but, having not seen him for over a week, I really thought he had regained his strength. But at the top of my steps his legs simply quit and he buckled and could not get up. I was afraid to let him sit down—he was on his knees. So, there we were. Since I am sort of small, I was helpless. I thought about the sudden burst of strength that folks get in times of extreme stress but thinking didn't do it, I got no stronger. Finally, between me and the newell post of the staircase and Ben pulling we made it shakily into my bedroom and a chair. What a fright!

Then it hit me. What was an eighty-four-year-old woman doing trying to teach an eighty-one-year-old man the jitterbug turn? I started laughing. No one would believe that I had brought a man upstairs to do that. Or, sadder still, maybe they would.

Ben is a stubborn rascal and, since both of his daughters were attending a New Years Eve party, I couldn't call them. He insisted on driving himself home. He made it and called me at each stair landing on the way to his bedroom. I wondered then if it was time to forget men friends.

Just when you think the world, anyway my part of it, has deteriorated and gone to the bad place, things turn around.

Last night at dinner, one woman at my table had vertigo, so she
didn't feel like talking and the other is deaf as a post and she can't
hear enough to talk back and partake. Also, I'm not the best company.
So, that's the setting when this most attractive lady came in, with the
priest at a near table, wearing a black and red close fitting hat that
reminded me so much of a hat I bought in Rome, Italy almost fifty
years ago that I could not stop looking at her when she took it off.

So, when I started to leave, I stopped by her table to tell her
how great she looked in it. She said it was just too hot. And I know
it was, even though it had been snowing some off and on all day (a
big surprise for Atlanta). She and I started to talk and she told me
about a book she was writing about a little girl who died and, of
course, turned into an angel. I told her that Dana was specializing
in writing children's books and, of course, I couldn't leave mine out.

Her book was mixed up in dreams and angels—sounds like
it should be a charming one and one that Dana will love hearing
about. One thing brought on another. So, I asked her if she had
ever taken a dream class. She was taking one now. It was so exciting
to learn about her course, the same one I took in 1985 when I had
breast cancer, which she has now and is going to the same class
being taught by the same teacher I had. We could not believe it, I
really got excited! She offered to drive me to the class to visit. It's a
cancer class for patients of Northside Hospital, the same set up. I
can't believe it!

Peggy, Anita and Dana came by today to see how happy I am
here. It is, I know, expensive as "all get up" here. They expect me to
be at my best, and I tried. Dana is as sweet as ever and so inquisitive.
I had forgotten how many questions that "one" may ask. She doesn't
really want to know how a person right at ninety-nine years old feels.
There just isn't any way – when you live around sick folks all the
time waiting for them to die, a guessing game – Who's next? I don't
think that way all the time, it's just better if you don't talk about it.

It's time to get on a more pleasant subject. Our new doctor did come day before yesterday on Thursday. I like him very much and hope he can get my problems worked out. I really believe he can.

The main problem in our family right now is Peggy. She is pretty sick and keeps putting off going to a doctor – I really don't believe she has one. I really don't want her to feel so bad, although I realize George will look after her if she will let him – she is pretty stubborn.

Since I have been sick, everyone at St. George's has been most attentive and I do appreciate their care, serving meals to my apartment and doing what they can to keep things nice, like emptying the trash, etc.

I went to our little dining room for breakfast—and hope I'll be going to lunch and the other meals. I'll know more about my health problems on Thursday. That's four days away. Come on four days, let's go! I want to be able to do more for Peggy. She is a sweet, precious daughter and does everything she can for me when I need her. I feel bad not being able to help her. I can tell by her voice that she is sick.

Mabel and Elsie. You don't say one without the other. They were my husband's sisters, a little bit different from most girls at the time. Their mother did not allow them to wear makeup and, I believe, frowned on boys, at least the dating kind.

But they did love their brother—and then, all of a sudden, he goes and falls in love with me! What a shock! To make matters worse, we elope! Why not? Everyone else was doing it. We, their darling brother and I, slipped off one weekend and did it! We sent telegrams to our families. What brats we were, without knowing it.

All hell broke loose for good reason. His father was sick with colon cancer. We saw them through that and then for years after Mabel and I had it around and around but recovered as our children came along. Children can accomplish everything and ours did. Mabel and I made up our differences and remained friendly from then until her death.

In the meantime, she married a fine man at around fifty years old. Even so, Mabel was not going to let us go. She bought a cemetery lot next to ours and has been near her brother for several years now. But I do have to say that Mabel was a good aunt to our children and they loved her.

Elsie grew up a little differently. Her life and the subject I am going to bring up are a little foreign to me, but when this is read in the future it won't be so strange as it is getting more and more prevalent, or perhaps I should say more people are coming out of the closet. For many years, long before Elsie was fully grown, it was obvious that she was more comfortable with girls than with boys. Or perhaps I should have said was thinking and acting more like a boy than a girl. Boys seem to know more about these things than girls because Wesley had already warned their mother that Elsie was getting too thick with a certain girlfriend of hers in the neighborhood, which was really not too strange since we all have best friends at certain times of our lives.

⚛

Here's something my grandson Matt says, which I think is a great lesson for all to bear in mind about life:
"Sometimes you get the bear, and sometimes the bear gets you."

⚛

They finally counted to ten.

The first time I went down was when the cheese grits boiled over in my clean oven. Everything was on time for my Christmas brunch, twenty-three or four of family, in-laws, children's in-laws plus a family of four from Russia (Tbilisi). I always feel generous and giving a few weeks before, the true meaning of Christmas, everyone is welcome. There's always a bed at my inn or a chair at my table.

I start weeks in advance, cooking and freezing. I overdid it this year. My little freezer was groaning and begging. Oh, well, what the heck! The entire family, some under duress, had agreed that we, especially me, were spending too much for family gifts. So, I planned to make my gifts the old-fashioned way, cookies, cakes, etc. I pored over cookbooks and really got some good things going. Little did I realize that come Christmas morning everyone would already be full of my food and each others', not to mention the parties. But this was weeks before Christmas and, besides, my weight was down.

I've always had the brunch, I suppose it's expected, it's just my thing to do. It's sort of like having a baby, you forget the pain and go again. This year I had had plenty of practice, a party for twenty-six that went off like clockwork, good food, great guests and, best of all, a young lady from the club to tend bar and help clean up. No problem, I can do the brunch just fine.

To get things off to a bad start, I awakened at 3:30 that morning and could not go back to sleep, had to think, remember to ice down the champagne, got to bring three bags of ice up from the freezer. Lord, I need a husband for things like that. All of that breakfast meat that would be sure to hasten everyone's death (except two grandchildren who were vegetarians) had to be brought up and warmed. What will I do first? Cook the cheese grits, butter the biscuits, fill the pitchers with orange juice and Bloody Mary mix. The bar was already set up, table set, really everything was on time. Then why couldn't I sleep? Best thing to do was to be dressed by six o'clock, couldn't stand for my children to see me unfixed. Good idea, then I won't be rushed. All right, who needs sleep anyway?

By seven-thirty things were indeed under control, the cheese grits were the best ever, two big Dutch ovens of them, mmm. You could really be neat if you emptied them into a large Pyrex dish and kept them warm in the oven. Then all of the pans would be washed. Good idea. Meats were wrapped in foil as were the biscuits, cranberry and bran muffins, rum cake was totally drunk, so was the raspberry sauce for the chocolate cheesecake, dishes and glasses for everything in the right places. Pretty proud of myself. I was on my feet, sparring right along, feeling strong and couldn't miss now.

Then the countdown began. Folks were due to arrive around ten-thirty. I was really on time, been up half the night, but so what, everything was beautiful. Made a last check around, turned on lights, run upstairs to spray on a little perfume, not too bad a hair day considering. Vanity, thy name is woman. That was the beginning of my mistakes. The cheese grits really got going and boiled over in my clean oven, calm yourself, plenty of time to clean that up. So, back in the Dutch ovens they went, okay, no problem. Now you had better put the crab imperial (we begin with something fancy) in to cook. By this time both ovens are crammed with different foods that need watching.

Now, where are the people—got to make this thing come out even. Woops, there they come. I didn't have children, I had wild people pouring in with packages.

"Have a Bloody Mary"

"No, we want champagne!"

They were messing up my game plan a little. I had planned champagne during the meal and dessert, that's fine, though, plenty of champagne. Coffee for the seventeen and eighteen year olds. "Sure it's made," just not in the dining room yet, it's right where I'm working. "No saucers, Granny, we don't use saucers, just cups." Oh, dear, at that time I was wavering a bit, perhaps the referee counted to six. I recovered. Everyone was screaming and yelling. I couldn't tell whether they wanted me knocked out or what. I guess they were just acting as their normal wild selves.

Time to serve the crab and at the same time get all of that food into the dining room. The only dish to behave was the huge, beautiful fruit platter, quiet and serene, just perfect, nothing I could do to ruin that.

Not so with the sausage, as it warmed the bottom got a wee bit dark, sort of black, "Oh, me". How could you forget it did that the last ten Christmases? Well, I had too much anyway. Just as I was into all of that, someone came up behind me and gave me a big, sexy hug. No time for sex! So, without thinking, me, the calm, sweet, kind one, said, "Go away." The referee was counting eight and one-half. I was groggy, gasping for air. Again I recovered. I never thought I could.

After the gifts were exchanged and my house was half-trashed, the referee came out and counted to ten.

We've pretty well covered the folks of the past, those that have gone on. And, do you know, they are going to be a tough act to follow. They were the ones that did not always play by the rules, so they were prone to be the most interesting. That is not to say we would all like to be them, to follow exactly what they believed or to copy their ways. Times were different then and we all more or less live by the time that we live in.

Now I want to tell you about some folks of the present—my children, grandchildren, great-grandchildren, and great-great-grandchildren, plus the folks some of them married.

Elaine, my firstborn, is now seventy-seven years old. She takes very good care of herself, stays with the times, and therefore looks and acts much younger. Her life has not always been easy even though it started and remained good during her growing-up years. Thanks to her daddy she had just about anything she wanted—anyway, everything she needed—and was loved by all of the family. Elaine was always pretty, had many friends, and was popular throughout her life. She was also bright from the beginning and stayed that way. She knows most of the answers. And when she doesn't, she finds them. But all was not happiness, mainly because her first and second marriages were not successful. She had three wonderful boys, two by her first marriage and one by her second; Mark, Lee and Tom.

Elaine has always made a good home for her family. She loves to entertain and does it beautifully. Even though her two marriages were not completely happy, she didn't ruin her life trying to stay in them after she saw a way to end them. After all of these years she has managed to build a happy time for herself and to let her boys make their lives happy. Elaine's boys are grown. Mark is fifty-seven, happily married to Susan, and several times a grandfather. Tom loves his job and is doing well. Unfortunately, Lee died of diabetes at forty-two years of age. He was such a sweet boy from the very beginning. After Elaine's divorce from Buddy, Lee and Mark came with Elaine to move in with us for about a year. Getting them into new schools was another thing—Lee we placed in Pace Academy (a private school on West Paces Ferry, very close to us), but Mark could not get in because his class was full, so he went to Birney Elementary. Anyway, I was a young mother again. Our child, Peggy, was twelve at that time and was in another private school, Lovett. What I'm getting at is I had three schools to drive children to. And do you know, it worked. We had Nellie working for us full-time helping me. What a godsend she was! She played a major part in our lives back then.

Elaine has been in love with Pat Monaco for years and, even though they have not lived together as if they were married, it has been a satisfying time for her and for Pat. They like to travel and find a lot of things to make life good for each other. Money does not seem to be a problem as they both have enough. So, all is well with her—except that her beautiful condominium in a lovely part of Atlanta was flooded during several days of rain. It is being repaired but, since the walls and flooring were badly damaged, it may take two or more months before she can move back in.

Sometimes you heard someone talk about Elaine or Anita, but usually it would come out either Anita and Elaine or Elaine and Anita, most always together.

Let me tell you about Anita and her family. She is my middle daughter. She came home one afternoon after teaching school telling us about a young man (a Marine) who had been asked to talk to her class, which he did. She was impressed enough to go out with him. That was the beginning of big things. It got serious enough for them to get engaged and then married. Anita was a member of Wieuca Road Baptist Church where she wanted the wedding to take place. Anita, Wesley and I got busy. Anita's piano teacher meant a lot to her and she wanted him to take over the music, but it didn't work; he and the lady with the beautiful voice could not get going with the music. We decided, with Anita's approval, that her daddy would do the hard part, fire the piano teacher, and I would get a player from the church. It worked! Anita was relieved and happy.

The wedding was beautiful, everything about it was perfect; the bride beautiful, groom handsome, and both families so pleased. Guy (the groom) decided to give me, or I should say our family, a Weimaraner puppy that grew overnight to be quite a large dog, sort of like a horse and not well behaved. I took him to training school and got well trained. That is, I got well trained, not the dog.

This marriage has been perfect. It has been fifty-four years now and they have proven to be a wonderful couple, great parents and grandparents. They have both climbed their individual ladders, successful in everything they did. Guy is and has been a good builder, a three-term state senator and well known in Dahlonega. They have both been very active in the school system in Georgia.

The best part of this marriage has been and is their wonderful daughters, Dana, Lisa and Sally. Dana is a writer now specializing in children's books, has had several published and more in the works. Dana is married to Pete, a writer and editor with many other talents. They live in Los Angeles, CA. Lisa is married to Robert and they also live in California. They have two lovely daughters, Karyn and Kathryn. Kathyrn is a little tag along, she is eleven and a real sweetie—also busy, busy! She'll probably end up being an actress or something of that sort. Both girls are beautiful and smart. Karyn, Anita's granddaughter, is married to Brandon. Their wedding was a real beauty, different for our family in that it was a military wedding. Karyn and Brandon are graduates of North Georgia College in Dahlonega and he plans to remain in the military. Sally has been in the school system for years. She is so tiny she looks like one of the students instead of a teacher or counselor, but she is very good at what she does. Sally is married to Graham and they have two children, Will and Sam, who are thirteen and ten and who keep the family busy with soccer.

All of Anita's girls lived with me in Atlanta for several months either before or after graduating from college: Dana with her first job at Public T.V., Lisa while in school at one of the hospitals studying to be a nurse, and Sally doing her student teaching in an Atlanta high school. Goodness, what a large, productive family we have. I am proud of each of them.

I must add this bright note; our family seems to be on top of it all, and everything they attempt turns out well. It sounds as though all of these good things happen without effort, but that's not so, they also put in a lot of hard work. It helps make it a little easier by each of them being smart and knowing what they want to accomplish and to set their goals and stick with them. They also help each other. Anita and Guy help Sally and Graham by taking care of Will and Sam when needed and some when not needed. They love the boys and the boys love them. It's an ideal setup since they all live in a sort of compound. These boys will always feel loved and will never want for anything. All of this goes for Kathryn and Karyn, too. What great grandparents they have!

Sam is next, my third child. He was an average all around boy, wanted to do and be everything. Then at around eleven years old he developed juvenile diabetes. What a tragedy that was! From then on life was not only miserable for him but for the entire family. Wesley did not understand this terrible disease any more than I did even though he tried. Between us and several others we formed a Juvenile Diabetes Association that met first in our home having a doctor meet with us. That went on for awhile. Then, as far as we were concerned, it fizzled out. Atlanta was not very well equipped as far as specialists were concerned. We just didn't know what to do for help. We both, Wesley and I, became nervous wrecks. Our family life suffered, our marriage was not the same. Wesley did not know how to deal with Sam's fear, which was real, and I'm sure I pulled in the opposite direction. Just writing this brings back unhappiness. This went on until the college years came. UGA at that time was somewhat of a party school that Sam's life did not fit in with. What a healthy young man could do, Sam could not. He tried, but oh, the results! In his second year when he was home for a weekend his eyes hemorrhaged and that was the beginning of the end of his life. He only lived to be thirty-one years old. However, some of those years were happy ones; he met a pretty girl, Judy, and they were married for five years. They lived in Hartwell, Georgia located in the beautiful Georgia mountains and lakes and were very happy. He sold real estate for a man named Ralph Olds who he had known for some time.

Then there's Peggy, the baby of the family. What a colorful life she is living! She also attended UGA and met a handsome fellow named Jim Dawson. They fell in love and rushed through college in three and a half years so they could be married, which they were, and soon had two children, a boy, Matt, and a beautiful little girl, Laura, both darling children that I got well acquainted with by helping Peggy with them while she worked. She worked hard and was very successful at several different things. She was a court reporter for years and ended up owning her company. It was hard work but she managed very well and helped Jim send the children to private school, Holy Innocents' Episcopal. They received a good education, finished with top grades, and went on to college; Laura to art school in Portland, Oregon, and Matt to music school in Dallas, Texas. Laura fell in love with a young man in Portland named Brent, and brought him back home. They had a sweet little talented boy, Ned. Shortly before Ned was born, Jim tragically and suddenly died. Peggy was alone for several years and then George Edwards came into her life. They married and George has fit in well with the family and has been very helpful to me.

After six years, Laura and Brent decided to call it quits and separated, later divorcing. All turned out well in the end. Laura found out that art was a hard way to make a living for her and a child, so she decided to attend nursing school and that proved to be a wise choice because she is an excellent nurse, and also because she met Jesse, who is a handsome, bright and very kind young man who is also good with Ned. They really fell in love and married in a fairytale wedding, their back yard filled with lights. You just wouldn't believe how beautiful it was, just perfect, weather just right, not too cold and everyone in a festive mood, children running around having fun, folks making pictures. Laura and Jesse worked hard. Laura made huge marshmallow chandeliers along with little tiny strings of lights laid all over their big back yard by Jesse. What a lovely sight, the bride beautiful and Ned and Jesse so handsome! After much fun, everyone went to the next-door yard for the ceremony which was simple but beautifully done in front of a rock background, and then back to the bride and groom's yard with kids throwing baby marshmallows along the way. How about the food? Plenty served in and around the kitchen and beautifully done dining room. Can you imagine?

❧

Dear Grandchildren,

Let me think. I came to Atlanta to live with my grandmother when I was fourteen years old; that was in 1931. Coming from Melbourne, Florida (a very small town on the east coast of Florida), a small nothing but fresh air and oranges kind of town, to a big city like Atlanta was thrilling.

So many things that we take for granted now were simply not around then. Oh, sure, automobiles were around but not everyone had one, certainly not two or three. Street cars were the main way of getting around town. I loved riding them. They had a certain smell, I thought. A big city smell, not unpleasant, a really good, dependable way to get where you needed to go. They loaded and unloaded folks every block or so, pretty handy, good for young folks, got them home on time because they only ran until midnight. Black people sat in the back and got off at the back door. Only whites could sit in front, which seemed natural then. We've come a long way!

So many things were invented since that time, and we got to enjoy each new thing as it came along. Refrigerators for one; before that we had iceboxes, ice was delivered every day or so. Most homes had a radio (one) and what a great source of entertainment – Kate Smith (singer), Amos and Andy (comedians), Red Skelton (comedian), dance marathons where people danced for days nonstop, never resting except when they slept leaning on their partner. Crazy, but interesting and fun to listen to and big prize money for the winners.

Big bands were born then, Tommy Dorsey, Guy Lombardo, etc. Then along came Bing Crosby, later Frank Sinatra. That kind of music never died, it is still strong today, wonderful dance music.

Airplanes were not as we know them today, no jets, just prop planes. We couldn't believe the speed of jets later. Trains were the mode of transportation for the average (or not so average) person. Presidents had their own passenger cars, so luxurious. Movie stars traveled in class on those trains. Later, of course, on planes.

There were no dial telephones. You raised the receiver on an upright phone and the operator said, "Number please."

The Great Depression started in 1929 when the stock market crashed. Everyone felt it, some more than others. Hunger was commonplace, unemployment reigned. Farmers could not afford to farm. To sum it up, our country was in one big mess!

Even so, my life as a teenager was not bad after I came to live with my grandmother. She made a fair living as a chiropractor. We were for the most part pretty safe. Crime has always been, but it seems that back then you had to look for it. Now it looks for you. Drugs and alcohol were not prevalent. Oh, sure, on older boy on occasion might have something to drink. I was just not around any of that. Besides, I married when I was eighteen and we could barely afford a Coca-Cola every now and then. My husband, your grandfather, was a hard worker and made a good salary for those days, eighty dollars a month, which very soon was raised to one hundred.

However, enough about my life. Some great people passed through our world back then, people who changed our thinking and will always be remembered as courageous people.

Charles Lindbergh, everyone knows his story, his brave, determined flight across the ocean, the terrible kidnapping of the baby son. I remember seeing that cute little blond, curly haired child's pictures in every newspaper for weeks. Everyone grieved.

President Franklin Roosevelt brought this poor, hungry country back on its feet and instilled patriotism and the will to fight and to win in all of us. We all had to sacrifice, but not like the young men who fought in World War II. President Roosevelt had what he called "Fireside Chats" from time to time. He used this time to keep the country informed as best he could of what was going on with the war. What was it he said? "We have nothing to fear but fear itself". Always very inspiring. He was a most dynamic leader. With his charisma, his power to convince and to persuade, he rallied the country and, by golly, we won the war. He did all of this through radio and newspapers, also through public appearances. What could he have done with television?

I'm sure you've read or heard of the big three, Roosevelt, Churchill and Stalin. They would have secret meetings usually at sea for safety reasons. As I remember, the big one was in Yalta.

Keep in mind, at that time I had three little children and, even though they had not invited my husband to join the forces early on, they finally did. That's how bad we were faring. His company, Cotton Producers (later Gold Kist), needed him to run a warehouse in Savannah (defense plant). So, after he was called, he was sent from Fort McPherson to Savannah for the duration. My brother, Hal, was a paratrooper and my brother, John, was a gunman. John was wounded and sent home. Hal was captured by the Germans on D Day and remained a prisoner for nine months. Five years later he died of a heart attack.

During the war women worked in defense plants of all kinds, built planes, etc. I was twenty-three years old at the beginning and had no one to keep my children. So, I stayed home feeling helpless.

These were scary times. At times, it seemed like we might lose the war. We had practice "blackouts," sirens sounded air raid wardens patrolled the streets to be sure all windows were blacked. We had dark light proof curtains.

It seemed to have taken a war to save our economy because after a few years, things started to look up and some form of prosperity has been with us ever since.

All of this happened a long time ago but I suppose some things stay vivid forever.

There is plenty more if I just dig.

Love,

Granny

This is a Sunday morning and I skipped church simply because I wanted to rest, to cut my hair, hem a few change of the season skirts, that sort of thing.

It seems much to my surprise that my thoughts, really serious thoughts, have taken a turn just this morning in my direction. Dana called (she is visiting her folks in Dahlonega, Anita and Guy) to ask me a question which had never occurred to me. However, since Anita's children are deep thinkers, it came up at the breakfast table. They get carried away sometimes—nothing wrong with that—but I did want to hem those skirts and I knew if I put off writing about this, it would lose its flavor. So, let's see what I can come up with. Oh, yes, the question. It was, why did my children call me mother? My first inclination when asked a question is to answer it in a hurry, never mind thinking it through or asking them why they asked, what's behind the thought or anything. I suppose I don't want to disappoint the asker, so I just say the first thing that pops in my mind and I'm stuck with that.

There are lots of reasons to call your mother "Mother" and, true to form, I only gave one, and, not true to my nature, it was a very negative answer, not the correct answer. I would have made a big, fat "0" on that test, had there been one. However, I'm sure that did not matter with Anita's group. They are very interesting, good discussions and all of that. If you want analyzing, just go for a meal. I love it and them. And, if I can get in a word, I hang in there with them. They started me thinking and, since that takes a little doing, they do not know the rest of my deep-thinking answer.

Now, let's think about the word "Mother." With the exception of "love," it is the most beautiful word in the English language, I think. Think about it. Does the doctor say, "Give the newborn baby to its mama or mom"? Not as a rule; it's to its mother, right?

Come to think of it, the reason we call our mothers what we do is usually the father's fault. When he gets tired of playing with or holding the sweet little one, what does he say? "Go to your mother, mom or mama." So, there it goes, he starts it. And that's not all, he usually continues calling her that dear name even after the children leave home. Then it turns into Granny, Grandmother, Nana or Grandmama. Whatever happened to Anita or Helen or some of the newer moms, mothers or mamas? Well, they also lose or change their original identity. Interesting ---

We had a 6:30 wakeup call this morning at St. George's by way of the fire alarm! Not too unusual – timing was a bit bad – false alarm ignored by most of us. One of these days it might not be, so it's best to be prepared.

St. George is a beautiful retirement village, brand new as of November, 2002. As a matter of fact, I was the third one to move in, the first in the North Building. All is well even though it has taken a little getting used to the concept of apartment living, going down to dinner every night, lots of wonderful people, etc. I suppose it is like being in a luxury camp for older folks. Anyway, this is the way to go. Even though I'm healthy, when I started adding up the years I've been around, they seem to go up instead of down. I'm getting my life back to sort of normal again, exercising one hour daily, keeping my weight down, going to church, getting more active in happenings around here. I've made lots of friends and seem to be included in activities, if I want to be. I can be friendly or a bit of a loner if I choose. It always seems to go back to free choice; doesn't it?

Something interesting happened to me yesterday (just in time, I might add, because for the first time in a long time I had allowed myself to become "stagnant." Some folks might call it bored.) Several days ago I took a book down from my shelves and started to read. It was called *The Frances Virginia Tearoom* and Peggy had found it in a bookstore several years ago and surprised me with it. The story behind this is that when I was sixteen years old during the Depression I worked for this famous tearoom (none like it in all of Atlanta, the most popular place to eat) as a counter girl.

This cookbook was written by the niece of one of three women that owned the Frances Virginia. Apparently, she is not a novice in the literary or the food field; she had quite a long history and resume. There was an address and telephone number listed on the front page of the book. So, I decided to call and talk to whoever was around. Not surprisingly, a voice mail came on. Not expecting to hear from anyone again, I forgot about it. Several days later I was surprised to hear from a very excited author named Mildred (Millie) Huff Coleman. I'm sure she thought everyone was long gone (dead) that was the least bit connected to the tea room. She plans to come out to St. George next Friday to interview me and to find out first-hand about the old beginning days of The Frances Virginia. There went my boredom!

There were four of us that were hired as counter girls, all of them older than I was. However, that did not matter, we all became friends. I remember each one of them. Emma Jane Reese seemed to be the one I knew best. She was cute looking, a bit bossy but a first-class worker. We had fun. I wish I could remember the names of the other two. I remember exactly how they looked, talked, laughed. I can still hear them.

The mother of one or more of the ladies who owned the Tea Room was cashier and hostess at first. Then very shortly business grew fast, so a new hostess was hired. We were used to the mother, so wondered about Ms. Rabi, the new hostess. Of course, she was charming, well qualified and very nice looking. It worked out well.

Everyone ate at the Frances Virginia. At first there was a small Tray Shop upstairs. Let's see, why was that? I believe at first she served afternoon tea and lunch. I know two sessions were included because we had a back room with cots so we could take naps if we wished while waiting between servings. Very shortly the Tea Room or Tray Shop was built and we moved down two floors away from the main dining room. It was a tremendous success right from the beginning. The kitchen was small and I believe they brought the food down from the main kitchen by a dumb waiter. They had two women and a young man named John, as I remember, in the Tray Shop kitchen.

The food was always on time. The hot tables and salad bars were never allowed to run too low, hot food was hot, cold food was cold, desserts, beautiful and delicious. But boys and waitresses kept things going at the tables as far as drinks, water, silver and dishes were concerned. All we did was to work the counters, serve and be polite. I remember our little speeches, "Will you have a salad? Would you like a dessert? Not salad or dessert?" Nothing too personal, always friendly, but not too, nice pleasant smiles. We liked our jobs. We were not called by our first names ever, Mrs. Beck, Miss Rabi, everyone called us by our last name, as Miss Murdoch (me), Miss Reece and so on. We had no restrictions as to our food, we could have anything we wanted. The ladies were very kind to us, but also firm. I remember after I married at eighteen my father-in-law was very ill, colon cancer, he had no appetite at all, in fact, was near death. Mrs. Beck kindly asked if I wouldn't like to take him food that might appeal since it was different and very tasty. I remember taking, among other things, smothered chicken. He liked it and I believe he started to like me, though he died before we became too well acquainted.

I worked there until I was three months pregnant. What days those were!

Looking back, I thought that first step was bad, took real courage. Little did I know! This whole life takes courage, I have found that out along the way. But how can you be brave if you have never been afraid?

I can't tell you how it's going to be the rest of the way, but I have an idea it's going to be fun. Tell you what, I'll let you know later.

# AFTERWORD

## THOUGHTS FROM HELEN'S DAUGHTERS

My Mother - She is my best friend.

We made many great trips together…. family vacations to Longboat Key and Sea Island (we were also partners in crime and did not always follow the rules. Sometimes we had a bloody Mary or two on the way down) We enjoyed trips to St. Simons, Rome, London and Morocco and a wonderful trip to the South of France.

Her expressions of advice to me were:

Anything that can't be done before midnight shouldn't be done.

Don't cry if you lose.

Where boys were concerned, if you don't like me, I don't like you.

There's something to be said for imperfection.

And most important… You can never learn to be brave if you have never been afraid.

There has never been a problem I couldn't share with her, and I always did. She gives good, solid advice, but be careful if she says, "Oh Pooh." That is not good! It is very good to be The One. Enjoy it while it lasts, maybe an hour, a day or if you're lucky, a week or so, but it's worth it to have been on the list.

She is a seamstress, dressmaker and designer of the highest degree. In the right time and place, she could have given Edith Head a run for her money. She designed our beautiful prom gowns. The prettiest girl always won, but often my sisters and I came in second - the 'cute girls' with the gorgeous dresses.

We took it for granted that she was the prettiest of all mothers. Our Daddy did not like or understand a C on a report card. I know, like her children and grandchildren, he would give our mother an A+ as a wife, mother and extraordinary lady.

*Elaine*

Growing up, I always thought that my mother was the most beautiful mother of all, a cross between Susan Hayward and Vivian Leigh. At the same time, I felt that she was the most capable person in my world. She could do anything.

First of all, she could whistle. Not loud ugly sounds, but she could whistle beautiful songs and ballads. I always enjoyed hearing her. And somehow, she could always sew. Even as small children she made us beautiful clothes.

She was also one of the most hard-working persons that I have ever known. Growing up on Clay Street, I remember her shoveling coal into the furnace, painting the dark woodwork white, washing and starching the curtains and hanging them through the house on curtain stretchers, and constantly hanging clothes on the line. Also, I loved the smell of the floors when she waxed them, which was often.

I remember her becoming the Cub Scout Leader for my brother Sammy's troupe (no one else would take the job.) But her motto was "The show must go on." As children, whenever we needed something, like cheerleading uniforms or choir robes, she was there to make it happen.

When we lived on Foxcroft Road, she and my dad thought that it was the perfect setting for a swimming pool. Mother didn't know how to swim, so at fifty, she went to the Y for swimming lessons. She developed a great backstroke.

Mother had a way of making each of us feel special. You might say, being The One. This she passed on to my children. All three of my girls lived with her for several months after they graduated from college. With each of them, this created a lasting bond.

Mother, we all love you.

*Anita*

Our mother has been a tremendous role model to all of us in so many ways. She has a unique knack for making each of us feel special, so much so that we have a friendly competition going about who will be "the one" today. One of her most admirable traits has been a steadfast love and devoted admirer of our father. One particular story that comes to mind happened many years ago. She and our father were in New York City and were in the process of exiting a cab in front of The 21 Club. While our father was paying the fare, my mother spotted Red Skelton going into the restaurant. She jumped out of the cab and ran up to Mr. Skelton and said, "Mr. Skelton, wait right there, I want you to meet my husband, Wesley." Her thinking was that this would be a treat for the famous comedian.

At the age of 60 our mother decided it was time to learn to play golf, a sport she took up with much enthusiasm and determination. She would play or practice virtually every day, except for Monday when the course was closed. Her hard work paid off and she played in and won golf tournaments both at home and in St. Simons and Sea Island. She has even credited golf with saving her life. She told me just the other day, "If somebody does not like St. Simons and Sea Island, they will not like heaven one bit." As much as she dearly loved golf, her family always came first. It was not unusual to see her riding around with a set of golf clubs in her car and two children's car seats in the back seat. She would play eighteen holes of golf and then make a mad dash to pick up grandchildren at school while their mother was at work.

This book is just one more example of her determination and persistence. It has been a work in progress for at least fifteen years. She has always had faith that it would be published. And so it has! What a wonderful gift she has given to her children, grandchildren, great grandchildren, great, great grandson and many generations to come.

*Peggy*

# ACKNOWLEDGMENTS

I could not have finished this book without the help of so many of my friends and, of course, my loving family. Let me name a few.

First my children. Peggy, for constant help typing—what a great job she has done. Peter and Dana, the most wonderful couple—just when I thought I had come to a stop, they came to my aid. Pete worked with Anita on the editing and found my publisher, Robert Barr. Without all these people, there would be no book.

I am grateful to Elaine for her "baby book," Matt for his bear story that we all use from time to time, Laura for her nursing advice and more, to Anita and Guy for stories that they tell about family and friends plus Guy's new book, McAdams. I am thankful to George for taking me needed places, paying for all of that gas, plus his time spent, and to Pat for advice and encouraging me along the way and for helping Elaine when I couldn't. What a friend!

Finally, Peggy again because she couldn't keep a secret, telling me about all of my nieces, nephews and grandchildren planning to come to the signing on April 9. Thank all of you!

Let's not leave out St. George and all of my friends that have continued to encourage me along the way. It has been a busy way!

A special thanks to my friend Ruth Farington. We were having dinner at St. George recently and a cute waiter was serving us. Ruth accused me of flirting with him. "I never flirt," I said. "Helen," said Ruth. "You were born to flirt." And there was the title I needed for my book.

Thank you all!

www.shadowridgepress.com